GUÍA ☆☆☆
DE CIUDADANÍA

A Step-by-Step Guide

LEARNING EXPRESS ®

NEW YORK

OCT 2408

Library of Congress Cataloging-in-Publication Data:
U.S. citizenship. Spanish
  Guía de ciudadanía.—1st ed.
    p. cm.
  ISBN: 978-1-57685-617-8
1. Citizenship—United States—Handbooks, manuals, etc. 2. Naturalization—
United States—Handbooks, manuals, etc. 3. Americanization—Handbooks,
manuals, etc. I. LearningExpress (Organization). II. Title.
JK1758.D4818 2008
323.6'230973—dc22

                                                    2007048379

Printed in the United States of America

9 8 7 6 5 4 3 2 1

First Edition

For more information or to place an order, contact LearningExpress at:
    55 Broadway
    8th Floor
    New York, NY 10006

Or visit us at:
    www.learnatest.com

OCT   2U09

CONELY BRANCH

CONTENTS

CIUDADANÍA ESTADOUNIDENSE

Una guía

- ◆ Saber qué esperar y cómo hacer una solicitud
- ◆ Aprender la materia relevante para el examen de ciudadanía
- ◆ Leer testimonios verdaderos de otra gente que ha salido bien en el examen
- ◆ Incluye nuevo formulario N-400

Cómo utilizar este libro

Cómo utilizar este libro

Felicitaciones—¡has decidido hacerte ciudadano americano! Mientras pensabas en buscar la ciudadanía, es cierto que te has dado cuenta de que es una decisión profunda. Esta decisión lleva algunas responsabilidades importantes. Pero antes de poder realizarlas y demostrar tu fidelidad a la Constitución de los Estados Unidos y a la gente americana, tendrás que participar en la naturalización—el proceso a través del cual los inmigrantes se hacen ciudadanos.

¡No te preocupes! Sí que la naturalización es un proceso complejo. Hay solicitudes que completar, entrevistas que hacer y exámenes que pasar. Con un poco de ayuda, sin embargo, ¡tu naturalización puede ser facilísima!

¿Sabes que . . .

... más de 10% de la población de los Estados Unidos nació en otro país? Lo que significa, claro, es que no eres la única persona ahora que se enfrente a la decisión de hacerse ciudadano. De hecho, éste es un país de inmigrantes; cuando seas ciudadano, estarás continuando una tradición americana muy antigua.

Aquí empieza todo

Este libro te dará la información y reglas básicas que necesitarás para hacerte ciudadano de los Estados Unidos. No es un substituto por la ayuda que te puede ofrecer un abogado. Para información sobre la manera adecuada de conseguir tal ayuda, lee el Apéndice B.

En el Capítulo 1, te harás familiar con todos los pasos que requiere la naturalización. Este capítulo incluye un horario para asegurar dónde estás en el proceso y adónde vas después.

> ☆ NATURALIZATION: el proceso de confirmar todos los derechos ciudadanos de un país

El Capítulo 2 explica cómo la gente se hace elegible para la ciudadanía y para la naturalización (sólo una de cuatro trayectorias hacia la ciudadanía). Esta información puede ser difícil, pero al seguir los pasos de que hay un resumen en este libro, será más fácil. Este capítulo explicará la manera exacta de determinar tu elegibilidad. También explica cómo conseguir ayuda legal si la necesitas.

> ☆ ELIGIBILITY: el estado de haber satisfecho todos los requisitos

El Capítulo 3 te dará detalles sobre los pasos necesarios al hacer una solicitud para la ciudadanía. Aprenderás a identificar los documentos necesarios, verás una solicitud ejemplar y te harás familiar con el proceso de naturalización.

¿Sabes que ...

... en los Estados Unidos, solamente ciudadanos tienen el derecho de votar? (Con una "tarjeta verde", "*green card*" se puede vivir, trabajar y asistir a escuelas estadounidenses, pero no se puede votar en las elecciones.)

El Capítulo 4 discute el elemento más importante de naturalización—el examen de ciudadanía. En este capítulo, encontrarás un resumen del examen—qué esperar y cómo prepararte. Encontrarás consejos útiles para estudiar y no preocuparte en el examen. Después de leer este capítulo estarás listo para practicar en el Capítulo 6, que contiene muchas preguntas ejemplares.

Como se hará evidente en las preguntas ejemplares, estudiar la cívica estadounidense será el aspecto más importante a través de tu preparación. Un repaso más o menos corto—que incluye historia, gobierno, cívica general e información sobre la Constitución—se contiene en el Capítulo 5.

Casos especiales y otras excepciones—por ejemplo, la ciudadanía dual—se discuten en el Capítulo 7. Para repetir: este libro no contiene consejo legal, sino que te ofrece la información fundamental y las reglas que seguir a través del proceso.

Hemos incluido muchos recursos para facilitar tu proceso de naturalización: el Apéndice A contiene una lista completa de oficinas USCIS. El Apéndice B contiene varios recursos útiles y una lista de organizaciones que te pueden ayudar. El Apéndice C contiene formularios ejemplares, y el Apéndice D contiene una lista de siglas, muchas veces difíciles que interpretar.

La inmigración: el porvenir

En el verano de 2001, George W. Bush, el presidente de los Estados Unidos, visitó Ellis Island, el puerto neoyorquino donde más de 12 millones de inmigrantes han llegado a este país. Puede ser un proceso largo hacerse ciudadano. Prometiendo acelerar el proceso, el presidente Bush dio la bienvenida a 29 ciudadanos nuevos en su ceremonia de juramento—su "swearing-in". Dijo, "La inmigración no es un problema que resolver, sino una señal de una nación de confianza y fuerza. Los recién llegados no deben ser tratados con sospecho ni resentimiento, sino con honestidad y cortesía".

Con la preparación adecuada, ¡pronto te encontrarás recitando el juramento de fidelidad a los Estados Unidos de América en tu propia ceremonia!

La naturalización— un resumen del proceso de hacerse ciudadano

EN EL AÑO DE 2004, casi 540,000 personas fueron naturalizadas como ciudadanos americanos. Completaron el proceso que tú ahora empiezas, probablemente con la ayuda de sus amigos, familias y otros recursos como este libro. Si el proceso de hacerte ciudadano a veces te parece demasiado complejo, quizás te calmará saber que hay muchos miles de personas en varios puntos del proceso también. Y ellos saben, como tú, que con preparación tendrán éxito.

La mejor manera de preparar es saber qué esperar. Este capítulo te dará un resumen de la naturalización en los Estados Unidos. Te dirá lo que debes hacer primero, y cuándo lo debes hacer.

¿Sabes que . . .

... la población hispana en los Estados Unidos es más grande en California, Florida y Tejas? Según recerca del año de 2004, el condado Los Angeles en California, con 4.6 millones de latinos, contiene la población más grande. El condado Dade en Florida, que contiene Miami y 1.4 millón de latinos, es el segundo. En el condado Harris en Texas, que contiene Houston, hay 1.3 millón.

Source: Bernstein, Robert. "Texas Becomes Nation's Newest 'Majority-Minority' State, Census Bureau Announces." U.S. Census Bureau News, Washington, D.C., August 11, 2005.

Paso 1

Determina tu elegibilidad. En general, tendrá el derecho de buscar ciudadanía si *uno* de los dos primeros casos y el último caso te aplica:

◆ Hace por lo menos cinco años que vives en los Estados Unidos legal y permanentemente.

◆ Hace por lo menos tres años que vives en los Estados Unidos legal y permanentemente mientras estás casado con un ciudadano americano durante todos los tres años.

◆ Has estado físicamente presente en los Estados Unidos por la mitad (por lo menos) de tu período de residencia legal y permanente.

Además, podrías estar elegible si

◆ Vives en los Estados Unidos legal y permanentemente y tu(s) padre(s) son ciudadanos americanos.

◆ Eres miembro de las Fuerzas Armadas de los Estados Unidos (Formularios. N-426 y G-325B se requieren también en este caso.)

Todo esto se discute más en el Capítulo 2.

   ☆ **GREEN CARD: una tarjeta de identificación que prueba el estatus de un inmigrante como "residente permanente" de los Estados Unidos**

Paso 2

Consigue un Formulario N-400 de los *U.S. Citizenship and Immigration Services* (USCIS). Este formulario es tu Solicitud para Naturalización. Para conseguir este formulario, puedes ponerte en contacto con la oficina USCIS más cercana, visitar su página de web (www.uscis.gov) o llamar a 1-800-870-FORM.

Paso 3

Junta tus materias de solicitud y envíalas a USCIS con el honorario apropiado y documentos de apoyo. Puedes entregar la solicitud hasta tres meses antes de tu fecha de elegibilidad. Tu solicitud consistirá en

- ◆ Formulario N-400.
- ◆ El honorario de $595 para la solicitud y otro de $80 para la huella digital. Estos dos se pueden pagar con un cheque de $675, dirigido a "U.S. Citizenship and Immigration Services". (Confirma los honorarios antes de enviarlos; estos precios corresponden al año de 2008, cuando se publicó este libro.)
- ◆ Tres fotos en color, 2″ × 2″ (disponibles dondequiera que se hagan fotos de pasaporte).
- ◆ Una fotocopia de tu tarjeta verde y del revés.

Paso 4

Hace que un oficial graba tu huella digital. Hazlo *después* de entregar tu solicitud. Después de que USCIS reciba tu solicitud completa, te enviará una carta para fijar una cita para la huella digital. Te explicará adónde ir, y cuándo. (USCIS tiene Centros de Apoyo [*Application Support Centers*] en la mayoría de áreas metropolitanas, y vehículos en que se graban la huella digital.) Lee la carta con cuidado. Además, lleva la carta contigo cuando vayas a la cita.

Quizás no entiendes por qué es necesario que el gobierno tenga tu huella digital. El FBI (la policía federal de los Estados Unidos) usará tu huella digital para hacer un "background check" criminal. Asegurará que eres de "buen carácter moral", una frase que se explicará en el capítulo siguiente.

Paso 5

¡Estudia, estudia, estudia! Has completado todos los pasos que corresponden a tu solicitud. Ahora puedes enfocarte en aprender más sobre la historia de los Estados Unidos y su gobierno actual. La entrevista contiene un examen sobre estos temas. Es preciso que estudies porque, para salir bien en el examen, tendrás que contestar correctamente por lo menos 70% de las preguntas. Los Capítulos 5 y 6 te ofrecen preguntas ejemplares y un resumen de la cívica americana. Utiliza estos capítulos, en conjunto con otros libros para el examen, cuando estés preparando. Una guía buena y comprehensiva se llama *Pasa el examen de ciudadanía, 3ra edición*, que editó LearningExpress.

Cómo, dónde y cúando estudiar

Puedes realizar tu plan de estudios al

➤ Identificar un lugar tranquilo.

➤ Utilizar luces fuertes para leer.

➤ Apagar la radio y la televisión.

➤ Pedir ayuda de tu familia y tus amigos.

➤ Organizar un grupo para estudiar.

Determinar tus objetivos y mantener un horario te ayudará a dominar la materia en el examen, puesto que sigas estos cinco consejos.

Paso 6

Asiste a tu entrevista y al examen oral. El USCIS te enviará una carta que especifique la fecha de la entrevista. Es normal si la fecha no ocurre hasta un año (o más) después de entregar la solicitud. Prepárate a proveer información actual—por ejemplo, si cambias de dirección o haces viajes fuera de los Estados Unidos—después de completar la solicitud.

Cuando asistes a la entrevista, prepárate a contestar preguntas sobre tu solicitud, ti mismo, tu familia, tu trabajo y sobre tu vida en general. Contesta todas las preguntas honradamente. El Capítulo 4 discute la entrevista con más detalle.

Paso 7

Si has salido bien en la entrevista y el examen oral, éste será el paso final—y el más emocionante—de todo el proceso. Recibirás una carta del USCIS que contenga la fecha y hora de su ceremonia de juramento, el *"swearing-in"*. En la ceremonia, dirás el Juramento de Fidelidad y recibirás tu certificado de ciudadanía.

Hay dos cosas importantes que tener presente a través del proceso. El primero es *siempre ser honrado*. Contesta toda palabra con la verdad—no mientas por lo que se refiere a tu condición, donde vives, crímenes, nada. El segundo: *siempre estar preparado*. Si has de completar el formulario N-400, reúne toda la información que se necesita antes de empezar. Haz copias del formulario y practica rellenarlo para prevenir errores más tarde. Si estás yendo a la entrevista, está seguro de que hayas preparado y repasado bastante la materia histórica y cívica.

Juramento de fidelidad: Si sales bien en el examen y la entrevista, recitarás (en inglés) este durante juramento la ceremonia:

Desde este momento, por juramento, declaro que absoluta y entera-mente renuncio toda fidelidad a cualquier príncipe, potentado, estado o soberanía de que o de quien he sido sujeto; que apoyaré y defenderé la Constitución y las leyes de los Estados Unidos de América contra todo enemigo, extranjero o doméstico; que demostraré verdadera fe y fidelidad al mismo; que tomaré las armas cuando la ley me lo requiera; que haré servicio en las Fuerzas

Armadas de los Estados Unidos cuando la ley me lo requiera; que haré trabajo de importancia nacional bajo la dirección civil cuando la ley me lo requiera; y que tomo esta obligación libremente sin ninguna reservación mental ni motivo de evasión; que Dios me ayude.

☆ **ABJURE: renunciar solemnemente**

☆ **FIDELITY: la calidad o el estado de ser fiel**

¿Qué significa el Juramento de fidelidad? Pues, en el primer lugar, significa que estás preparado a abandonar tu antigua identidad como ciudadano de tu país natal. Es un asunto serio, y es una cosa que tienes que considerar profundamente antes de empezar el proceso de hacerte ciudadano. Además, cuando declaras tu fidelidad a los Estados Unidos, quiere decir que apoyarás el país de cualquier manera, sin excepción—incluso si tienes que oponerte a tu país antiguo. Para alguna gente, es muy difícil hacer. A veces, quiere decir que tendrás que apoyar los Estados Unidos en una guerra—sea en el combate o en trabajo civil. Bajo circunstancias especiales, podrías ser elegido a hacer trabajo de "importancia nacional" a causa de tus orígenes nacionales o tus competencias específicas. Lo más importante es tener presente lo que estás prometiendo y estar preparado a hacer el juramento sin hesitación. Para entender más sobre tu nuevo país, lee la Constitución y la Declaración de Independencia, que se incluyen en el Capítulo 6.

Ya que tienes un resumen del proceso de naturalización, continúa leyendo sobre los *requisitos de elegibilidad* para la ciudadanía en el capítulo que viene.

☆ ☆ ☆
LA HISTORIA DE MIGUEL

TENÍA 16 años cuando mi familia y yo salimos de Colombia para ir a los Estados Unidos. Cuando llegamos a Nueva York, me parecía que fuera una película. Había todo tipo de gente en la calle, como había imaginado. En ese momento supe que me gustaría mucho vivir en los Estados Unidos. Después de un rato no demasiado largo aprendí el inglés, y mi profesor de "English as a Second Language" en el colegio me ayudó mucho.

Cuando empecé a trabajar, me di cuenta de que no ser ciudadano fue un obstáculo grande. Un día cuando regresaba a casa de mi trabajo como portero, me detuve en la Biblioteca Pública de Nueva York y busqué información sobre lograr la ciudadanía. Estuve muy en conflicto con respecto a la idea de hacerse americano–amo mi patria, Colombia–pero había pasado la mitad de mi vida en los Estados Unidos y sabía que en cualquier otro lugar, si alguien me preguntaría de dónde era, le contestaría "los Estados Unidos". Entonces, decidí hacerlo. Busqué algunos libros en la biblioteca que me ayudaron a través del proceso; y mi hermana Daniela, que se había naturalizado unos años antes, también me ayudó mucho. Me enteré de que había varias organizaciones sin fines lucrativos que ayudan a candidatos con asuntos legales, estudiar para el examen, y mucho más.

Es importante saber que todas las materias y la gente atenta no te ayudarán si no haces un esfuerzo de 100% hacia el proceso de hacerse ciudadano. No tiene que ser super-difícil, pero hay muchos detalles y, desafortunadamente, mucho papeleo y mucho tiempo haciendo colas; puede ser un proceso tedioso. Pasaron 16 meses entre el ponerme en contacto con el USCIS y la ceremonia de juramento, pero hay variación según el caso. Mi consejo principal es esto: completa la solicitud correctamente tan pronto como posible y usa el resto del tiempo disponible para estudiar. Quizás 16 meses te parezca muy largo, pero hay casos en que se requiere mucho más tiempo. No sabía nada de la historia americana, y como resultado necesité todos los meses para estudiarla. El aspecto del examen que me asustaba más fue memorizar los nombres de los nueve jueces de la Corte Suprema; mi aspecto favorito fue aprender varias citas de patriotas de la Revolución Americana de 1776. En general, me encantó estudiar, y el proceso me inspiró a repasar la historia de Colombia otra vez.

A fin de cuentas, la entrevista oral fue más fácil de lo que esperaba, y la ceremonia de juramento fue más solemne. Estoy muy orgulloso de poder decir que soy estadounidense.

Requisitos preliminares

DETERMINAR TU ELEGIBILIDAD puede ser una de las partes más confusas del proceso de naturalización. También es una de las más importantes. Si no estás elegible para la naturalización, *no puedes hacer una solicitud para la ciudadanía.* Este capítulo te explicará los requisitos de elegibilidad. Algunos requisitos pueden ser confusos a primera vista; éstos se discutirán en más detalle.

Es necesario que tengas al menos 18 años.

Este requisito es bastante claro. Si tienes menos de 18 años, no estás elegible y tendrás que esperar. Los hijos de ciudadanos estadounidenses, por otra parte, en algunos casos pueden derivar la ciudadanía de sus padres.

Es necesario que seas residente permanente de los Estados Unidos y que tengas una Tarjeta de Residente Permanente (Permanent Resident Card; *antiguamente* **"Alien Registration Card"** *y frecuentemente llamada una* **green card).**

Si no has recibido ni una *Permanent Resident Card* ni una *green card*, entonces no eres residente permanente y no puedes completar una solicitud. Si crees que eres residente permanente, pero no tienes una *Permanent Resident Card*, debes ponerte en contacto con la oficina USCIS más cerza de ti. Está seguro de que hayas conseguido correctamente el estatus de residente permanente.

Es necesario que haga al menos cinco años que seas residente permanente (tres años si estás casado/a con un ciudadano estadounidense).

Si hace cinco años que eres residente permanente, eres elegible y tienes una *Permanent Resident Card*. Si hace entre tres y cinco años que eres residente permanente, eres elegible solamente si TODO lo siguiente es verdad:

◆ Estás casado, y vives, con un ciudadano estadounidense.

◆ Has sido esposo del ciudadano por la duración de los tres años anteriores (o más).

◆ Hace al menos tres años que tu esposo es ciudadano americano.

◆ En los 18 meses anteriores, no has salido de los Estados Unidos.

Si no son verdades todos los cuatro, y si hace entre tres y cinco años que eres residente permanente, entonces no estás elegible.

Si hace *menos* de tres años que eres residente permanente, entonces no estás elegible. Además, si has pagado impuestos federales con el IRS como *nonresident alien*, es posible que los oficiales decidan que hayas renunciado tu estatus de residencia permanente; es probable, entonces, que estarías inelegible.

Dentro de los cinco años anteriores, es necesario que NO hayas estado fuera de los Estados Unidos por más de 30 meses.

Los abogados de inmigración dicen que éste es uno de los requisitos más confusos según sus clientes. En efecto, se requiere que estés físicamente presente en los Estados Unidos por la mitad, al menos, del período en que seas residente permanente. Se requiere, para estar elegible, que seas residente permanente por cinco años, o 60 meses. De esto, tienes que haber estado presente por, al menos, 30 meses—la mitad.

Para determinar si estás elegible, reúne los registros en que has detallado todos los viajes que has hecho en los cinco años pasados. Si, después de añadir todo, has pasado menos de 30 meses fuera de los Estados Unidos, estás elegible. Si no, tu fecha de elegibilidad se pospondrá hasta que haga 30 meses de los 60 anteriores que estés presente en los Estados Unidos.

Vamos a mirar la situación de María, por ejemplo. Recibió estatus de residente permanente el 1 de julio de 2001. Si no pasara más de 30 meses fuera de este país entre ese día y el 30 de junio de 2006, estaría elegible el 30 de junio de 2006. Por otra parte, si ella viajó a su país natal tres veces hacia un total de 32 meses, no estaría elegible el 30 de junio de 2006.

Aquí simplificamos cómo se pospondría su fecha:

1 de julio de 2001: recibe estatus de residente permanente

1 de agosto de 2001 a 30 de septiembre de 2001: viaja fuera de los EE.UU

1 de febrero de 2002 a 31 de julio de 2002: viaja fuera de los EE.UU

1 de septiembre de 2002 a 31 de enero de 2003: viaja fuera de los EE.UU

1 de enero de 2004 a 31 de julio de 2004: viaja fuera de los EE.UU

1 de marzo de 2005 a 31 de agosto de 2005: viaja fuera de los EE.UU

1 de diciembre de 2005 a 31 de enero de 2006: viaja fuera de los EE.UU

Hasta el 30 de junio de 2006 (cinco años como residente permanente), María pasó 28 meses fuera de los Estados Unidos. Por consecuencia, si no hiciera ningún viaje más, estaría elegible el 30 de junio de 2006.

Desde haberte hecho residente permanente, es necesario que no hayas hecho un viaje individual fuera de los Estados Unidos de más de un año. (Se recomienda que no hagas ningún viaje de más de seis meses.)

Si viajas fuera de los Estados Unidos por un período de más de un año, es necesario que tengas un reconocido "Application to Preserve Residence for Naturalization Purposes" (Form N-470). Si no lo tienes, estás inelegible.

EXCEPCIONES

Es excelente que el gobierno ofrezca el formulario N-470 para preservar tu estatus de residencia si tienes que pasar un período largo fuera del país, pero no siempre se aprueba el formulario. Es posible que, si tienes que salir por más de un año, tengas que comenzar de nuevo el proceso de lograr cinco años de residencia permanente.

Es necesario que hayas sido residente por los tres meses anteriores del estado o distrito en que pretendes hacer la solicitud para ciudadanía.

No hay ninguna calculacóin difícil aquí. Si no cumples con este requisito, tendrás que esperar hasta que sí. Mientras esperas, puedes preparar tu solicitud de tal modo que esté lista cuando haga tres meses que vivas en tu estado o distrito.

Es necesario que seas capaz de leer, escribir y hablar un inglés básico.

Hay tres excepciones:

◆ Si tienes más de 50 años y hace más de 20 años que vives en los Estados Unidos desde hacerte residente permanente.

◆ Si tienes más de 55 años y hace más de 15 años que vives en los Estados Unidos desde hacerte residente permanente.

◆ Si tienes una minusvalía médica que impide que te pueda cumplir con este requisito. Si es así, tendrás que conseguir una "Medical Certification for Disability Exceptions" (Form N-648).

Es necesario que puedas tener éxito en la sección de cívica del examen oral.

Hay excepciones aquí también:

◆ Si tienes más de 50 años y hace más de 20 años que vives en los Estados Unidos desde hacerte residente permanente.

◆ Si tienes más de 55 años y hace más de 15 años que vives en los Estados Unidos desde hacerte residente permanente.

◆ Si tienes una minusvalía médica que impide que te puedas cumplir con este requisito. Si es así, tendrás que conseguir una "Medical Certification for Disability Exceptions" (Formulano N-648).

Por favor, lee el Capítulo 4 para más información sobre las secciones de lengua y cívica del examen oral.

Es necesario que seas una persona de buen carácter moral.

En este caso, ¡no hay excepciones! Si tu carácter moral se puede cuestionar, es probable que no estés elegible. Ten presente que no vale para nada mentir sobre tu carácter ni sobre crímenes en el pasado. Cuando ofreces la huella digital, el FBI conseguirá una historia personal a través de un *criminal background check*.

> ☆ **MORAL CHARACTER:** el conjunto de los atributos que componen y distinguen a una persona

La lista siguiente contiene ejemplos de cosas que deslucirían tu buen carácter moral:

◆ Cualquier crimen contra una persona con intención de hacer daño

◆ Cualquier crimen contra la propiedad o el gobierno que implica fraude o mala fe

◆ Dos crímenes o más para los cuales la sentencia agregada fue cinco años o más

◆ Violar una ley narcótica (de *controlled substances*) de los Estados Unidos, de un estado o de otro país

◆ Embriaguez habitual o conducción en estado de embriaguez

◆ Juego ilegal

◆ Prostitución

◆ Poligamia (estar casado con más de una persona al mismo tiempo)

◆ Mentir para lograr beneficios inmigratorios

◆ No pagar el sustento de menores o la pensión alimenticia

◆ Reclusión en una cárcel o una prisión por más de 180 días durante los cinco años anteriores (tres años si estás solicitando como esposo/a de un ciudadano)

◆ No completar un período de libertad provisional o condena condicional antes de hacer la solicitud para naturalización

◆ Si un juez ha mandado que seas deportado, no estás elegible para la ciudadanía. Si todavía te disputas en un juicio, no puedes aplicar hasta que hayas terminado y que tengas el derecho de quedarte en este país.

◆ Actos de terrorismo
◆ La persecución de cualquier persona por razones de raza, religión, origen nacional, afiliación política o grupo social

> ☆ **FRAUD:** un acto de decepción o falsa representación

Si eres hombre, tienes que registrarte con Selective Service. Para estar elegible para naturalización, es necesario que una de las siguientes condiciones sea verdad:

◆ Eres mujer.
◆ Eres hombre registrado con *Selective Service*.
◆ Eres hombre que no llegó a los Estados Unidos de ningún modo hasta después de tener 26 años.
◆ Eres hombre nacido antes del 1 de enero de 1960.
◆ Eres hombre que vivía en los Estados Unidos entre las edades de 18 y 26 años, pero que no registró con *Selective Service*; tendrías que enviar una carta con tu solicitud, una "*Status Information Letter*", a *Selective Service* que explique por qué no registraste.

> ☆ **SELECTIVE SERVICE:** un sistema bajo el cual los hombres se eligen para hacer servicio militar

Si eres mujer, no tienes que preocuparte de este proceso de registración. Si eres hombre, por otra parte, sí que tienes que hacerlo. Aplica solamente a los hombres que entraron en los Estados Unidos *de cualquier estatus* antes de tener 26 años. Para algunos hombres, esto es más confuso que el requisito de presencia física: *status* puede significar una persona que busca asilo, un refugio, un no inmigrante con visa y otras clases.

Entonces, la ley federal requiere que todo hombre que tenga entre 18 y 26 años se registre con *Selective Service*. Aplica a *todos* los hombres que viven en los Estados Unidos.

Este requisito *no* quiere decir que te estás haciendo miembro del militar. A muchos inmigrantes parece que es así. Registrar sólo quiere decir que estás notificando al gobierno estadounidense quién es y cómo contactarte en caso de emergencia nacional. Incluso en el caso de una guerra u otra emergencia, todos los hombres no serían elegidos a servir.

¿Sabes que . . .

... si eres miembro de las Fuerzas Armadas, podrías estar elegible para la ciudadanía después de sólo tres años de residencia permanente? Además, tu solicitud (N-400 Military Naturalization Packet) se considera más rápidamente, el que hace más corto el proceso entero. Para más información, ponte en contacto con un oficial del USCIS.

Si entraste en los Estados Unidos antes de cumplir 26 años, tienes que registrarte para estar elegible para naturalizarte. Además, si entraste en los Estados Unidos antes de cumplir 18 años, tienes que registrarte dentro de 30 días después de tu cumpleaños. Si no lo has hecho, *hazlo ahora*. Estás violando la ley si no lo haces.

Para registrarte, consigue los formularios en la oficina de correos más cercana—o visita el sitio de Web de *Selective Service*: https://www .sss.gov/RegVer/wfRegistration.aspx.

Si te has registrado, tienes que incluir tu número de *Selective Service* en la solicitud. Si no lo sabes, puedes llamar a 1-847-688-6888.

Si tienes 26 años o más de edad y no cumpliste con el requisito de registrarte con Selective Service, tienes que contactarlo directamente. Lo puedes llamar a 1-847-688-6888, y tendrás que contestar unas preguntas para recibir un "*Status Information Letter*".

Si un hombre no se registra con Selective Service, como dice la ley, se le niega:

➤ ciudadanía estadounidense (si la está buscando)
➤ trabajo federal

➤ prestados y otros dineros para la universidad
➤ formación profesional de JTPA (*Job Training Partnership Act*)

Es necesario que no seas, y nunca hayas sido, desertor de las Fuerzas Armadas de los Estados Unidos.

Si saliste de una rama de las Fuerzas Armadas antes de ser puesto en libertad, eres desertor y no puedes buscar la naturalización.

Es necesario que nunca hayas recibido una exención o licencia de las Fuerzas Armadas por ser extranjero.

Si es así, no estás elegible para la naturalización.

Es necesario que estés dispuesto a desempeñar servicio militar O civil para los Estados Unidos si la ley lo requiere.

Si tus creencias religiosas impiden tu participación en servicio militar, tendrás que estar dispuesto a hacer servicio no militar. Tendrás que enviar una carta que explique por qué tus creencias te impiden. Explícalo exacta y honradamente. En la carta, debes pedir un Juramento de Fidelidad modificado.

☆ **PROHIBIT:** impedir; causar que alguien no haga algo

Si USCIS acepta tu petición, harás el juramento sin decir "to bear arms on behalf of the United States when required by law".

Es necesario que apoyes la Constitución de los Estados Unidos.

Esto siempre se llama "attachment to the Constitution". Al apoyar o aliarte con la Constitución, dices que estás dispuesto a apoyar los Estados Unidos y la Constitución. Declaras tu apoyo cuando dices ". . . I will support and defend the Constitution and the laws of the United States of America against all enemies, foreign and domestic, that I will bear faith and allegiance to the same . . ." en el Juramento de Fidelidad.

Es necesario que comprendas y estés dispuesto a tomar un Juramento de Fidelidad a los Estados Unidos.

¡No eres ciudadano antes de tomar el Juramento! Es buena idea familiarizarte con el Juramento de Fidelidad. Practica las palabras para estar cómodo y entender lo que significan. Si te sientes que no puedas, en buena fe, recitar el Juramento, entonces no estás listo a convertirte en ciudadano estadounidense.

¿Sabes que . . .

... la ley estadounidense asigna 226,000 *green cards* cada año en la categoría de inmigración familiar? La razón es que USCIS procesa las solicitudes de familia directa más rápidamente que los de familia indirecta. Según USCIS, los extranjeros pueden emigrar a los Estados Unidos "a través de" un familiar. Los parientes directos reciben tarjetas verdes al llegar; los indirectos muchas veces esperan unos años antes de recibirlas. "Directo" quiere decir: esposo/a de un ciudadano, hijo soltero (con menos de 21 años) de un ciudadano, padre de un ciudadano, o ciudadano estadounidense con más de 21 años de edad).

Si has leído este capítulo y todavía tienes preguntas sobre tu elegibilidad, utiliza los recursos que se enumeran en los Apéndices A y C. Si todavía no está claro, quizás debes ponerte en contacto con un abogado que se especialice en la inmigración. Un sitio de Web es www.law guru.com. Ofrece consejo por un honorario único, y pueden responder a varias preguntas gratis. Cuando entiendas tu estatus de elegibilidad, lee el Capítulo 3 para información sobre completar la solicitud N-400.

☆ ☆ ☆
LA HISTORIA DE BRIGIT

HACE COMO 25 años que vivo en los Estados Unidos. Mi familia vino a los Estados Unidos de Inglaterra cuando tenía ocho años. Adaptarme a Nueva York después de vivir en el campo inglés fue una experiencia definitivamente difícil para una niña. El primer día de escuela en los Estados Unidos, me parece que todos los alumnos estadounidenses pretendían imitar mi acento británico, y yo pensaba, "No tengo acento extraño, sino ¡Uds. lo tienen!" Pero hablar inglés al llegar absolutamente me ayudaba a adaptarme. Me gustaba crecer en los Estados Unidos, pero nunca pensé en hacerme ciudadana hasta la elección presidencial de 1996. Tenía 25 años y había hecho una vida propia aquí. La elección me iba a afectar directamente, pero al no poder votar, no tuve ninguna voz en la elección. Fue en ese momento que decidí hacerme ciudadano.

Comenzar fue el aspecto más difícil del proceso de solicitud. Primero, llamé al USCIS. Pronto me enteré que fue difícil conseguir información por teléfono. La página de Web fue mucho más útil: entré mi información en los formularios y los imprimí. Entonces, esperé una carta que explicara el siguiente paso. Mi mejor consejo es: ten paciencia y haz preguntas si las tienes.

Por lo que se refiere al examen, el mío fue una entrevista oral de sólo diez preguntas, y no tuve que escribir. Estudié mucho para la entrevista, pero las preguntas a fin de cuentas fueron más o menos fáciles. Creo que el proceso duró 11 meses en total. La ceremonia de "*swearing-in*" fue excelente. Tuvo lugar en Brooklyn con unas 400 otras personas de todo país. Me enteré de que ¡tienen tres ceremonias a la semana, cada una con 400 personas! Todo el mundo estaba muy bien vestido, y claro que la familia de cada ciudadano nuevo estaba allí.

El discurso del juez fue muy bueno: dijo que las únicas hojas de papel que ador-
nan su pared eran el certificado de naturalización de su abuelo y la carta que lo
confirmó a él mismo como juez. A pesar de considerar todo el proceso un rollo
burocrático hasta ese punto, me afectó muy emocionalmente la ceremonia, y
tengo gusto en haberme hecho ciudadana estadounidense.

Cómo hacer la solicitud para la ciudadanía

HAS DECIDIDO convertirte en ciudadano estadounidense y has determinado que sí estás elegible. El siguiente paso necesario es completar una solicitud.

En primer lugar, necesitas un formulario N-400: "Application for Naturalization". Tendrás que ponerte en contacto con USCIS para conseguir este formulario. Puedes buscar la oficina más cercana, llamar a 1-8000-375-5283 o mirar la página de Web en www.uscis.gov para cargar los formularios. Puedes rellenarlos en la computadora y después imprimirlos.

VENTAJAS DE NATURALIZACIÓN

➤ El derecho de votar en elecciones federales, estatales y locales

➤ Protección contra ser deportado; los ciudadanos estadounidenses no pueden ser deportados

➤ La habilidad de viajar con un pasaporte estadounidense; tendrás que solicitar visas con menos frecuencia

➤ Más oportunidades de empleo; algunos trabajos, incluso en el gobierno, requieren la ciudadanía estadounidense

Completar el Formulario N-400

Para el año de 2002, el USCIS ha publicado una versión completamente nueva del N-400. Todas las versiones anteriores ya son inaceptables; asegura que estés usando el formulario actual. Un formulario ejemplar se incluye en el Apéndice C. Es buena idea familiarizarte con el formulario. Quizás te gustaría hacer unas copias para practicar rellenarlo. Así estarás seguro de que tengas toda la información requisita. El formulario que envíes al USCIS debe ser preciso, pulcro y sin errores. La página de Web de USCIS contiene un formulario que se puede imprimir: está bajo "Forms and Fees" en www.uscis.gov.

Parte 1: Tu nombre

La primera parte te pide el nombre y apellido actuales y legales. Si el nombre que aparece en tu *Permanent Resident Card* es diferente de tu nombre legal (incluso si se escribe mal), tienes que notar esta situación en la pregunta B. También te pedirá que incluya cualquier otro nombre que hayas usado. Además, cuando una persona se naturaliza, tiene la opción de cambiar oficialmente su nombre. Hay más información sobre esta opción en la Guía de Naturalización de USCIS.

Parte 2: Base para la elegibilidad

Aquí se te pide que elijas la manera de que estés elegible. ¿Hace al menos cinco años que vives en los Estados Unidos como residente permanente y legal? ¿Hace tres años y estás casado con un ciudadano? ¿Tienes *qualifying military service*? (Marca sólo una opción en la Parte 2.)

Parte 3: Información sobre ti

Esta parte pide información básica: la fecha en que te hiciste residente permanente, fecha de nacimiento, país natal, número de Seguridad

Social y número de registro como foráneo (*alien registration number;* "*A-number*") que aparece en tu *alien registration card.* ¿Estás casado? ¿Eres hijo/a de ciudadanos estadounidenses? Y si necesitas ayuda especial a causa de alguna minusvalía, aquí lo tienes que mencionar. ¡Contesta toda pregunta honradamente!

Parte 4: Direcciones y números de teléfono

Esta parte pide tu dirección de casa (y tu dirección postal, si las dos son distintas). También tienes la opción de dar tu número de teléfono y tu correo electrónico.

☆ **A-NUMBER:** tu alien registration number

Parte 5: Información para la búsqueda de historia criminal

El FBI usa esta información, en conjunto con tu huella digital, para buscar tu historia criminal.

Parte 6: Información sobre tu residencia y estatus de empleo

Completa esta parte con los detalles sobre los cinco años pasados. Contesta específica y honradamente. Enumera empleos y direcciones según una orden cronológica inversa, empezando con los más recientes.

Parte 7: Tiempo fuera de los Estados Unidos

Tendrás que saber detalles específicos sobre tu historia de viajes para contestar estas preguntas. Tendrás que incluir información sobre todo viaje fuera de los Estados Unidos, incluso los que duraron sólo un día, para el período de cinco (o tres) años anteriores de tu solicitud. Puedes adjuntar más hojas si se requieren. Si hay algún viaje de más de seis meses, prepárate a explicarlo.

Parte 8: Información sobre tu historia marital

Si estás casado, tendrás que proveer información sobre tu esposo/a: su nombre, dirección, fecha de nacimiento, país natal, ciudadanía y número de Seguridad Social. También tienes que proveer su *A-number*, estatus inmigratorio y de naturalización, si se aplican. Si tú o tu esposa se casó antes con otra persona, tendrás que proveer información sobre esto.

Parte 9: Información sobre tus hijos

Aquí tendrás que enumerar a tus hijos, si los tienen: sus nombres, sus fechas y países de nacimiento, ciudadanías, A-numbers y direcciones.

Parte 10: Preguntas adicionales

En esta parte hay 39 preguntas para determinar si hay otros factores que afecten tu elegibilidad. Éstas complementan las de la Parte 2. Has de contestar cada una con "sí" o "no". Tendrás que enumerar toda organización, club, grupo, etc., de que has sido miembro. Si no has sido miembro de ningún grupo, puedes contestar con "no". En esta parte también encontrarás una serie de preguntas, "*Oath Requirements*", que examina tu nivel de fidelidad a los Estados Unidos. Si tu respuesta a una de estas seis preguntas es "no", tendrás que explicar por qué. Otra vez: contesta cada una honradamente.

Es esencial proveer respuestas honradas. Es preciso entender las preguntas, en primer lugar, y dar respuestas correctas.

Parte 11: Firma

¡Firma tu solicitud! No se aceptará si no está firmada.

Parte 12: Firma de la persona que prepara el formulario, si no eres tú mismo

Si alguien te ayuda a preparar el formulario, es necesario que firme la solicitud también.

Parte 13: Firma en la entrevista

Es necesario que tú y tu entrevistador firmen el día de tu entrevista. *No* completes esta sección hasta que el entrevistador te lo diga hacer.

Parte 14: Juramento de Fidelidad

Al firmar la Parte 13, reconoces que estás dispuesto a tomar el Juramento de Fidelidad si se acepta tu solicitud. Como Parte 13, *no* completes esta sección hasta que el entrevistador te diga que lo hagas.

Después de completar el formulario, repásalo y asegura que hayas contestado honrada y completamente todas las preguntas. Escribe tu nombre y A-number en cualquier hoja adicional que hayas adjuntado a la solicitud.

(Es imprescindible que contestes *todas* las preguntas. Si no lo haces, es posible que USCIS tenga que devolverte la solicitud. Te tardaría todo el proceso.)

Tu carta de presentación

Tu carta de presentación debe enumerar toda la información que contiene tu solicitud. Se envías sólo un Formulario N-400, indícalo; si hay otros formularios, indícalos. Esto es tu oportunidad, además, para pedir que tu entrevista y tu examen tengan lugar el mismo día y en el mismo lugar que los de otro solicitante (si prefieres). Escribe el nombre y *A-number* de este solicitante.

En la página que viene, mira una carta de presentación ejemplar.

Antonio A. Gianninni
314 West 178 Street, #4R
New York, NY 10024
212-555-5434
Alien Registration #A0123456789

November 17, 2007

U.S. Department of Homeland Security
USCIS Vermont Service Center
Attention N-400 Unit
75 Lower Welden Street
Saint Albans, VT 05479-9400

To Whom It May Concern:

Please accept my enclosed and complete Application
for Naturalization. Included with my application you
will find a photocopy of my Alien Registration Card,
three color photographs as per your specifications,
and a check for $675 U.S. Dollars for the applica-
tion and fingerprinting fees, payable to the United
States Citizenship and Immigration Services.

If possible I would like to request that my interview be scheduled at the same time and place as my
wife, Alba Gianninni, #A0987654321.

I thank you for your time and consideration.

Sincerely,

Antonio Antonello Gianninni

Enclosures.

Paga

Por favor pregunta a los oficiales del centro de servicios más cercano; algunos prefieren que los cheques se dirijan al "U.S. Treasury". Tu paga consistirá en el honorario de solicitud ($595) y uno por la huella digital ($80). Se pueden combinar en una paga de $675. (Contacta a USCIS antes de enviar dinero para asegurar que el honorario requisito no ha cambiado desde la publicación de este libro.) Dirige tu cheque al "U.S. Citizenship and Immigration Services". USCIS *no acepta* efectivo. Envía sólo un cheque o giro postal. Sea tu paga un cheque o un giro postal, siempre tiene que ser apoyada por un banco o una institución que esté ubicado en los Estados Unidos. Es necesario que pague en dólares americanos.

Hay dos excepciones. Si vives en Guam, debes dirigir la paga a "Treasurer, Guam". Si vives en las U.S. Virgin Islands, se debe dirigir a "Commissioner of Finance of the Virgin Islands".

Fotografías

Tienes que presentar tres fotos de ti mismo con la solicitud. Desde el 2 de agosto de 2004, hay en efecto un cambio por lo que se refiere a los requisitos fotográficos: tienen que ser de un punto de vista totalmente frontal, como en un pasaporte. Deben ser en color, sacados dentro de los 30 días antes de presentar la solicitud y cuadradas (2 pulgadas cada borde). Se pueden sacar estas fotos en todo lugar donde se sacan fotos de pasaporte, por ejemplo la oficina de correos. Mira las páginas amarillas en la guía telefónica.

Específicamente, USCIS requiere que sus fotos:

- ◆ Sean idénticas
- ◆ Sean lustrosas, sin modificaciones ni marco
- ◆ Tengan un fondo blanco
- ◆ Entre barbilla y pelo midan 1 pulgada
- ◆ Se saquen de punto de vista frontal

Debes escribir tu nombre y *A-number* al revés de cada foto. Escribe ligeramente para no dañar las fotos. Hay más detalle sobre este tema en el folleto del Apéndice C.

Permanent Resident Card (Alien Registration Card *o* Green Card)

Haz una fotocopia de tu tarjeta—ambas caras. La copia debe estar bastante para que se pueda leer toda la información. Haz una fotocopia de tu información de pasaporte también.

RED TAPE

Muchas veces las agencias del gobierno tienen procedimientos muy formales y es poco obvio por qué existen. En los Estados Unidos, esta forma de burocracia se llama *red tape*. Puede ser frustrante encontrarse con *red tape*. Pero no pierdas la paciencia.

☆ **BUREAUCRACY: un sistema administrativo que adhiere rígidamente a muchas reglas**

Reunir tu solicitud

Antes de reunir y enviar tu solicitud, asegura que tengas todos los elementos requisitos. Sigue esta lista:

_____ Carta de presentación

_____ Formulario N-400, lleno

_____ Un cheque de $675 dirigido a "U.S. Citizenship and Immigration Services"

_____ Tres fotos en color, 2″ × 2″

_____ Copias de ambas caras de tu *Permanent Resident Card (green card)*

_____ Documentos de apoyo

_____ Un sello dirigido al "USCIS Service Center" que corresponde al estado donde vives

Una vez completada tu solicitud, debes fotocopiar cada página. Guarda las copias en un lugar secreto. Se recomienda que uses la opción de "*return receipt*" en la oficina de correos, o que pidas confirmación de reparto.

Adonde enviar tu solicitud

Hay cuatro *USCIS Service Centers* que aceptan el Formulario N-400. Adónde envías la solicitud depende de dónde vives actualmente. Usa la lista siguiente.

Si vives en

> Alabama
> Arkansas
> Carolina del Norte
> Carolina del Sur
> Florida
> Georgia
> Kentucky
> Louisiana
> Mississippi
> Nueva México
> Oklahoma
> Tennessee
> Tejas

Enviarás tu solicitud a

USCIS Texas Service Center
Attention N-400 Unit
P.O. Box 851204
Mesquite, TX 75185-1204

Si vives en

> Connecticut
> Delaware
> District of Columbia (Washington, D.C.)
> Maine

Maryland
Massachusetts
Nueva Hampshire
Nueva Jersey
Nueva York
Pennsylvania
Puerto Rico
Rhode Island
Vermont
U.S. Virgin Islands
Virginia
West Virginia

Enviarás tu solicitud a

USCIS Vermont Service Center
Attention N-400 Unit
75 Lower Welden Street
St. Albans, VT 05479-9400

Si vives en

Arizona
California
Guam
Hawaii
Nevada

Enviarás tu solicitud a

USCIS California Service Center
Attention N-400 Unit
P.O. Box 10400
Laguna Niguel, CA 92607-1040

Si vives en

Alaska
Colorado
Dakota del Norte
Dakota del Sur
Idaho
Illinois
Indiana
Iowa
Kansas
Michigan
Minnesota
Missouri
Montana
Nebraska
Ohio
Oregon
Utah
Washington
Wisconsin
Wyoming

Enviarás tu solicitud a

USCIS Nebraska Service Center
Attention N-400 Unit
P.O. Box 87400
Lincoln, NE 68501-7400

Después de haber enviado tu solicitud

Primero recibirás una carta de USCIS con la fecha y lugar de tu cita de huella digital. Si puedes, evita cambiar la cita; te retrasarás muchísimo. Lleva la carta contigo a la cita. También debes llevar tu

Permanent Residence Card y otra forma de identificación fotográfica. Discutiremos el proceso de sacar la huella digital en el capítulo que viene.

Cambiar de dirección

Es importante que notifiques a USCIS cada vez que se cambia tu dirección. Si no lo haces, todas las cartas de USCIS, por ejemplo la que especifica tu cita para la entrevista, se enviarán a tu dirección antigua. Se recomienda que no se traslade hasta que suceda la entrevista.

USCIS te dirá la fecha de tu entrevista y examen oral por medio de una carta oficial. Normalmente, la entrevista tiene lugar de seis a nueve meses después de que se reciba tu solicitud. Guarda esta carta, junta con las copias de tu solicitud, en un lugar digno de confianza.

El capítulo que viene te introducirá a varios tipos de preguntas que tendrás que contestar en la entrevista, lo que será un buen punto de partido para la preparación.

Consejos para juntar tu solicitud

_____ Escribe con letra de imprenta, o en el ordenador. Se recomienda que uses la versión "fillable" Adobe Acrobat en la página de Web.

_____ Repasa tu solicitud, buscando errores.

_____ Asegura que hayas rellenado todas las partes del formulario.

_____ Antes de enviar tu solicitud, haz copias de cada página y guárdalas.

_____ Dirige tu cheque a "U.S. Citizenship and Immigration Services". No envíes efectivo.

_____ Indica claramente, en el sello y en la carta de presentación, el tipo de formulario: "N-400 Application for Naturalization".

_____ Usa la dirección postal correcta.

_____ Junta todos los documentos de apoyo (y copias).

En tu entrevista con USCIS, tendrás que contestar muchas preguntas que se refieran a las respuestas que se dan en el Formulario N-400. A veces las respuestas correctas cambian entre el momento en que completas el formulario y el día de la entrevista. Está dispuesto a explicar cualquier diferencias, y haz una copia para repasar antes de la entrevista. Además, presenta una lista de todos tus viajes fuera de los Estados Unidos desde completar el N-400. Todavía tienes que cumplir con el requisito de *Physical Presence and Continuous Residency* hasta tu entrevista.

☆ **DISCREPANCY:** divergencia o desacuerdo entre hechos o aserciones; diferencia

Lista de documentos posiblemente requisitos en conjunto con tu N-400:

Todo solicitante tiene que enviar:

_____ Una fotocopia de ambas caras de tu *Permanent Resident Card*

_____ Tres fotos en color de tu cara de punto de vista frontal

_____ Un cheque o giro postal: $675

Si un abogado u otra persona te representa, envía

_____ Formulario G-28, "Notice of Entry of Appearance as Attorney or Representative"

Si tu nombre actual es distinto del que aparece en tu Permanent Resident Card, envía:

_____ El documento que confirma el cambio legal (licencia de matrimonio, confirmación de divorcio u otro documento de la corte) O una explicación detallada de por qué usas un nombre distinto

Si solicitas naturalización con el apoyo de estar casado con un ciudadano estadounidense, envía:

_____ Evidencia de que hace al menos los tres años pasados que tu esposo/a es ciudadano estadounidense (certificado de nacimiento, de naturalización, copia de la parte interior del pasaporte de tu esposo/a O Formulario FS-240 "Consular Report of Birth Abroad of a Citizen of the United States of America")

_____ Tu certificado de matrimonio actual

_____ Evidencia de haber terminado *todos* tus matrimonios anteriores (y de su esposo/a; divorcio o muerte)

_____ IRS Form 1722, que recompila información sobre impuestos para los tres años pasados; o una declaración de renta para los tres años pasados

☆ **DECREE:** un decreto que lleva toda la autoridad de la ley

Si has sido miembro del militar americano, envía

_____ Formulario N-426, "Request for Certification of Military or Naval Service"

_____ Formulario G-325B, "Biographic Information"

Si has viajado fuera de los Estados Unidos por seis meses o más desde hacerte residente permanente, envía

_____ IRS Form 1722, que recompila información sobre impuestos para los tres años pasados; o una declaración de renta para los tres años pasados

Si tienes esposo/a dependiente o hijos, y tienes que apoyarlos económicamente, envía

_____ Copias del decreto de la corte o del gobierno que los apoyas; Y

_____ Evidencia de que has cumplido con la corte o con el gobierno (cheques, recibos de giros postales, evidencia de saldos reducidos, etc.)

Si has sido arrestado o detenido por un policía u otro oficial y no había acusaciones, envía

_____ Una declaración oficial de la agencia responsable para indicar que no había acusaciones. Se recomienda, si te aplican estas condiciones, que consultes con un abogado.

Si has sido arrestado o detenido por un policía u otro oficial y *SI* había acusaciones, envía

_____ Los documentos originales, o copias autorizadas, para cada incidencia

Si has sido condenado o detenido en un programa de rehabilitación o "sentencia alternativa", envía:

_____ El documento de cada incidencia

_____ Evidencia de que completaste la sentencia (registros oficiales de probación, libertad condicional, etc.)

Si un arresto o condenación tuya fue quitado, sacado, rechazado, etc., envía

_____ El decreto original de la corte, o una copia autorizada, que confirma el rechazo de la condenación

☆ **EXPUNGED:** borrado, cancelado, rechazado

Si una vez no has logrado presentar la declaración de renta, contra la ley, envía

_____ Copias de toda tu correspondencia con el IRS sobre la incidencia

Si hay impuestos federales, estatales o locales que todavía tienen que pagar, envía

_____ Un documento firmado del IRS u otra agencia que reconoce que pretendes pagar los impuestos

_____ Documentos del IRS u otra agencia que demuestra el estatus actual de tu plan de repagar

Si solicitas, a causa de minusvalía, una excepción a participar en el examen, envía

_____ Formulario N-648, "Medical Certification for Disability Exceptions", rellenado por un médico o psicólogo clínico (la página de Web USCIS contiene una lista de médicos autorizados por USCIS.)

Si no te has registrado con _Selective Service_ y 1) eres hombre, 2) tienes más de 25 años, y 3) vivías en los Estados de 18 a 26 años bajo otro estatus de "no-inmigrante legal", envía:

_____ Una _Status Information Letter_ de _Selective Service_ (llama a 1-847-688-6888 para más información)

Si estás seguro de que estás dispuesto a aceptar todas las responsabilidades que lleva el hecho de hacerse ciudadano de los Estados Unidos, estás listo a comenzar el paseo hacia la ciudadanía. Claro que tienes primero que determinar que eres elegible; después, tienes que conseguir y completar el Formulario N-400. Antes de intentar rellenar este formulario, debes juntar toda información sobre ti mismo desde llegar a los Estados Unidos: certificados de matrimonio, certificados de nacimiento de tus hijos (si los tienes), documentos del gobierno, etc. Es importante saber tu *A-number*, y los de tu esposo/a y tus hijos. Si eres hombre con de menos de 26 años de edad, asegura que estés registrado con *Selective Service*. Si no estás registrado, *no estás elegible*. Lo más importante, como siempre, es contestar estas preguntas honradamente. Y no tengas prisa cuando completas el formulario. Lee las instrucciones con cuidado y saldrás bien. ¡Buena suerte!

☆ ☆ ☆

LA HISTORIA DE RAVI

Decidí salir de India y venir a los Estados Unidos cuando tenía 25 años. Me asustaba la idea de salir de mi familia y mis amigos para ir a un país enorme donde no conocía a ninguna persona. Mis padres se preocupaban de que fuera solo, pero como niño he oído varias historias de gente que se trasladaron de India a los Estados Unidos y tuvieron mucho éxito. Quería hacer lo mismo, y cuando lograra todo lo que esperaba, pediría que mis padres vinieran también. Había aprendido inglés como niño y me relajaba saber que, al menos, podría comunicar con otra gente cuando llegara en Nueva York.

Fue muy difícil los primeros meses, pero me enteré de que había una comunidad india muy grande en Nueva York, y conocí a mucha gente de todo país del mundo. Toda esta comunidad inmigrante había venido a los Estados Unidos con el mismo sueño que yo, y mucha gente me ayudó, como otra gente había hecho para ellos unos años antes. Durante mis primeros años aquí, trabajaba por las noches en cualquier empleo que pudiera encontrar, y asistía a la escuela durante los días. A veces tenía dudas de que sobreviviera, pero salí bien y hoy soy farmacéutico con mi propia familia. Puse, a fin de cuentas, comprar billetes para que mis padres vinieran a este país. Ellos estaban muy orgullosos de mí. Nunca se me olvidará la cara de mi padre cuando llegó—eso en si validó toda la pena.

Viví en los Estados Unidos 27 años antes de decidir convertirme en ciudadano. Este país se había hecho mi verdadera casa—quería poder votar, viajar como estadounidense sin tener que buscar visas y, cuando fuera necesario, planear mi jubilación. Hablé con unos amigos que habían completado el proceso, y me dijeron que fuera a una oficina USCIS. Fue difícil entender todo el papeleo. Tenía miedo también de salir mal en la sección histórico de la entrevista, entonces estudiaba con un libro que me prestaron unos amigos ciudadanos. El estudiar mucho, el entender la Constitución y el aprender la historia americana fueron mis partes favoritos de todo el proceso. Pero no había nada más impresionante que ver las caras felices de otros ciudadanos nuevos en la ceremonia de "*swearing-in*". Fue en ese momento que verdaderamente me di cuenta de que había realizado mi sueño. El consejo más importante que puedo comunicar a un solicitante es empezar prontito. Es importante y vale la pena.

La entrevista USCIS y el examen oral/ Preguntas ejemplares y respuestas

DESPUÉS DE HABER completado el proceso de naturalización, tendrás que esperar: USCIS te contactará con respeto al siguiente paso.

Después de que se presente el Formulario N-400

En general, pasan unos meses antes de que tengas noticias de USCIS. Si no has escuchado nada después 90 días, es buena idea llamar a 1-800-375-5283 para asistencia y para asegurar que hayan recibido tu solicitud.

En muchas instancias es normal que USCIS te llame o escriba para más información sobre ti, o si tus respuestas son confusas de alguna manera. A veces USCIS te puede devolver la solicitud si le falta información. Si USCIS te contacta, es importante responder dentro del período admisible. Si no lo haces, se puede abandonar tu solicitud.

Cuando USCIS te contacte, refiere a la copia del N-400 que has guardado. Guarda también tu número de recibo de solicitud, que te ayudará a mirar el estatus de tu caso en https://egov.uscis.gov/cris/jsps/index.jsp.

Huella digital

Haz todo lo que puedas para ir a tu cita de huella digital en la fecha y hora que ha determinado USCIS. De vez en cuando USCIS organiza un día "*make-up*" para solicitantes en situaciones especiales. En distritos urbanos, sin embargo, podrías esperar por demasiado tiempo y debes evitar esta necesidad.

Tu huella digital entonces se envía al FBI para inspección. Llevará a cabo una investigación de tu historia criminal, en los Estados Unidos tanto como en países extranjeros; también verificará más seguramente la información que escribiste en el N-400. Esto también puede requerir de 60 a 90 días; ten paciencia.

Con permiso del FBI, recibirás una notificación de la fecha y hora de tu entrevista. La fecha puede ser un año después del día actual, hasta dos años y medio. Trata seriamente de estar presente el día que se te asigna.

¿Sabes que . . .

... del año 1990 a 2000, la población asiática de los Estados Unidos creció de 72%? Ahora hay casi 12 millones.

La entrevista USCIS

Ten presente que la entrevista no existe solamente para examinar tu conocimiento de la historia y del gobierno estadounidenses. El entrevistador también tiene que averiguar

◆ Que tu Formulario N-400 esté acurado.

◆ Que tengas buen carácter moral.

◆ Que puedas leer, escribir, entender y hablar inglés.

Sin embargo, si tienes una exención del aspecto lingüístico, se notará en tu registro y el entrevistador no te examinará en esa área.

Qué llevar a tu entrevista

Aunque es normal estar nervioso, ten presente que si has estudiado bastante para la entrevista, no te tendrá que preocupar de nada. Un aspecto de preparación es juntar todas las cosas que necesitarás en la entrevista: los originales y las copias de todos los documentos relevantes. Tienen que ser versiones certificados, y tienen que ser documentos en inglés. Si están escritos en otra lengua, alguien los ha de traducir. La persona que los traduce no puede ser amigo, familiar u otra *interested party.*

➤ Identificación fotográfica

➤ *Permanent Resident Card*

➤ Pasaporte

➤ Documentos para viajar (de USCIS)

➤ Copias de declaraciones de renta de los cinco años pasados

➤ Tarjeta de registración de *Selective Service* (si eres hombre)

➤ Documentos que pertenecen a arrestos, juicios o probación

➤ Si vas a tomar un Juramento de Fidelidad alternativo, necesitas documentos de apoyo (por ejemplo de tu grupo religioso)

➤ Evidencia de haber apoyado a todos los hijos con menos de 18 años que viven fuera de tu casa (cheques cancelados, giros postales, etc.)

Como avanza la entrevista, verás que una parte de la información puede haber cambiado desde que enviaste el N-400. Es normal; el oficial notará los cambios y procederá seguirá haciendo la entrevista. No hay ninguna razón de mentir sobre un cambio de empleo o dirección.

Ten presente que, mientras contestas las preguntas, el oficial no sólo está averiguando tu información; está calificando tu habilidad de entender y hablar inglés.

Después, el oficial de USCIS te dará una selección de preguntas sobre la historia y cívica estadounidense. (La lista completa de preguntas oficiales aparece en el Capítulo 6.)

Hacer un plan de estudios

Para pasar la entrevista oral, es importante seguir un plan cuando te preparas.

Paso 1: Fijar un horario

Debes esperar preparar de seis a doce meses.

Paso 2: Tener la información correcta

Buscar las fechas en que son esperados varios documentos. Lee todo lo que reciba de USCIS.

Paso 3: Junta todas tus materias

Consigue libros de repaso, o cualquier cosa adicional que podrías necesitar. *Pasa el examen de ciudadanía americana* de

LearningExpress es buen ejemplo de un libro útil. Si tienes acceso al Internet, puedes buscar información en línea también. Busca cursos preparatorios en tu comunidad.

Paso 4: Haz un programa de estudios

Verás abajo un ejemplo de tal programa. Rellénalo.

Paso 5: Mantente fiel al plan y recompénsate

Por medio de un paseo por la tarde, una chocolatina o una llamada, es buena idea tener un sistema de recompensa. No es fácil estudiar tanto, y es preciso divertirte de algún modo mientras estudias.

Haz un programa:

Cuando sabes la fecha de tu cita, contesta las preguntas siguientes.

El examen es: _____

_____

Lo tomo el día: _____

_____

A esta hora: _____

_____

El examen tiene lugar aquí: _____

_____

Mis tres preguntas principales sobre el examen son: _____

_____

Intento estudiar así: _____

_____

Seis meses antes del examen: _____

_____

Cinco meses antes del examen: _____

_____

Cuatro mese antes del examen: _____

_____

Tres meses antes del examen: _____

_____

Dos meses antes del examen: _____

_____

Un mes antes del examen: _____

_____

Dos semanas antes: _____

_____

Una semana antes: _____

_____

Dos días antes: _____

_____

Un día antes: _____

_____

Saludos y conversación trivial

En la oficina de USCIS, el entrevistador te llamará e irás a una sala. Antes de empezar, iniciará alguna conversación muy general—"small talk"—para averiguar tu nivel de fluencia en inglés. Si se siente que no pueda comunicar contigo en inglés, es posible que termine la entrevista. Aquí se encuentran unas preguntas ejemplares de tal "*small talk*".

Preguntas "¿cómo estás?"

Q: How are you?

A: I am <u>fine</u> / <u>good</u> / <u>great</u>. OR <u>Fine</u> / <u>Good, thank you</u>.

Q: How is the weather today?

A: The weather is <u>fine</u> / <u>good</u> / <u>cold</u> / <u>warm</u> / <u>sunny</u> / <u>rainy</u> / <u>windy</u>. (Pick which one applies.)

Q: How did you get here today?

A: I came by <u>car</u> / <u>bus</u> / <u>subway</u> / <u>train.</u> OR <u>My son</u> / <u>daughter</u> brought me.

"Por qué estás aquí?"

Q: Do you understand why you are here today?

A: <u>Yes</u>.

Q: Why are you here today?

A: <u>For my citizenship interview</u>. OR <u>Because I want to be a U.S. citizen</u>.

Q: Why do you want to become a United States citizen?

A: <u>Because I love America</u>. (¡Usa tu propia razón!)

Empezar la entrevista

Q: Do you have any questions before we begin?

A: <u>No</u>.

Preparar y estudiar

Q: Have you prepared for the citizenship test?

A: <u>Yes</u>.

Q: Have you studied for the citizenship test?

A: <u>Yes</u>.

Q: How did you study / prepare?

A: <u>I read a book</u>. OR <u>I took a class</u>. OR <u>My children helped me</u>.

Juramento de honestidad

Entonces el entrevistador te pide que tomes un juramento. Te pide que jures a dar información honrada a través de la entrevista. Estas oraciones se podrían incluir. Dilos en voz alta varias veces para practicar.

Entrevistador:	"Ok, let's begin. Please stand and raise your right hand".
Lo que haces:	Levántate y levanta la mano derecha.
Lo que significa:	Estás listo para tomar un juramento.

Entrevistador:	"Do you promise to tell the truth and nothing but the truth so help you God?" OR "Do you swear that everything you say will be the truth?"
Lo que haces:	Di en voz alta, "Yes".
Lo que significa:	Has prometido contestar honradamente. Has prometido no mentir.

Entrevistador:	"Please sit down". OR "You can sit down now".
Lo que haces:	Siéntate.
Lo que significa:	El juramento ha terminado.

Práctica extra

Q:	Do you understand what an oath is?
A:	<u>Yes, it is a promise to tell the truth</u>.

El entrevistador entonces averiguará tu identidad, y tendrás que mostrar tu información, por ejemplo la *Appointment Notice* y *Alien Registration Card*.

Entrevistador:	"At this point, I have to check your identity. I need to see your **Appointment Notice** or **Invitation to Appear**. I would also like to see your passport if you have one, and your *Alien Registration Card*".
Lo que haces:	Muéstrale la carta que recibiste por correo de USCIS—tu **Appointment Notice** o **Invitation to Appear**. Entonces, muéstrale tu **Alien Registration Card**.
Lo que significa:	Eres capaz de probar quién eres.

Después de que el entrevistador ha confirmado tu identidad, la entrevista misma se puede comenzar.

Preguntas y respuestas típicas que se refieren al N-400

Tu entrevistador repasará tu formulario N-400 para averiguar la información que escribiste. Guarda una copia del N-400 para confirmar las respuestas.

Partes 1 y 2: Tu nombre e información sobre tu elegibilidad

Q: What is your name?

A: My name is _____.

Q: Spell your last name.

A: __-__-__-__-__-__-__-__-__-__-__-__-__

Q: When did you first come to the United States?

A: I came to the United States on _____ (mes, día, año).

Q: How long have you been a permanent resident?

A: _____ years

Q: Have you ever used a different name?

A: <u>Yes</u>. / <u>No</u>.

Q: Do you want to change your name?

A: <u>Yes</u>. / <u>No</u>. (Si lo quieres cambiar, especifica qué nombre prefieres.)

Q: To what do you want to change your name? OR
What name do you want to have now?

A: _____.

Q: What other names have you gone by? OR
What other names have you used in the past?

A: _____ OR None.

Q: What was your maiden name?

A: Before I was married, my name was _____.

Parte 3: Información sobre ti

Q: How long have you been a permanent resident of the United States? OR

How long have you lived in the United States?

A: _____ years

Q: When did you become a permanent resident? OR

When did you first come to the United States? OR

On what date did you enter the United States?

A: _____ (mes, día, año).

Q: You've been a permanent resident since _____,

is that correct?

A: <u>Yes</u>. (Si no, di la fecha correcta.)

Q: Where did you enter the United States? OR

What was your port of entry? OR

In what port of entry did you arrive in America?

A: _____.

Q: What is your date of birth? OR

What is your birthday? OR

When were you born?

A: I was born on _____ (mes, día, año).

Q: What is your country of birth? OR

Where were you born?

A: I was born in _____ (country).

Q: What is your nationality? OR

What is your current citizenship?

A: I am _____ (nacionalidad).

Q: What is your Social Security number?

(Quizás NO quieras escribir tu número de Seguridad Social en este libro, pero debes de todos modos memorizarlo).

A: My Social Security number is __ __ __ - __ __ - __ __ __ __.

Q: What is your marital status?
A: I am (<u>single</u> / <u>married</u> / <u>divorced</u> / <u>widowed</u>).

Q: Are you married?
A: <u>Yes</u>. / <u>No</u>.

Q: Have you ever been divorced?
A: <u>Yes</u>. / <u>No</u>.

Q: How long have you been married?
A: I have been married for _____ years.

Parte 4: Dirección y números de teléfono

Q: What is your home address? OR
Where do you live?
A: I live at _____.

Q: What is your home phone number? OR
What is your telephone number at home?
A: My phone number is __ __ __-__ __ __-__ __ __ __.

Q: Do you have a work telephone number?
A: <u>Yes</u>. / <u>No</u>. OR No, I am not currently working.

Q: What is your work phone number?
A: My work phone number is __ __ __-__ __ __-__ __ __ __.

Parte 5: Información para la investigación de historia criminal

Q: What is your height? OR
How tall are you?
A: I am _____ feet, ____ inches tall.

Q: What is your weight? OR
How much do you weigh?
A: I weigh _____ pounds.

Q: What is your race?

A: I am <u>White</u> / <u>Asian</u> / <u>Black or African American</u> / <u>American Indian or Alaskan Native</u> / <u>Native Hawaiian or Other Pacific Islander</u> / <u>Other</u>: _____.

Q: What is your hair color? OR
              What color is your hair?

A: My hair is <u>black</u> / <u>brown</u> / <u>blonde</u> / <u>gray</u> / <u>white</u> / <u>red</u> / <u>sandy</u> / <u>other</u>: _____. OR
              <u>I am bald</u>.

Q: What is your eye color?

A: My eyes are <u>brown</u> / <u>blue</u> / <u>green</u> / <u>hazel</u> / <u>gray</u> / <u>black</u> / <u>other</u>: _____.

Es posible que tu entrevistador te pida respuestas detalladas a las preguntas siguientes. Pero es posible también que sólo lea lo que has escrito en el N-400 y te pregunte si está correcto. Es preciso que conozcas extensivamente la información en tu formulario N-400. Si la información cambia, está dispuesto a explicarla.

Parte 6: Información sobre tu residencia y empleo

Q: Where have you lived in the past five years?

A: I have lived at _____ (enumera todas las direcciones, empezando con tu dirección actual).

Q: Are these all the places you have lived in the last five years?

A: <u>Yes</u>. / <u>No</u>. (Si no, explica por qué no lo escribiste en el formulario).

Q: Have you lived in any other places in the last five years?

A: <u>Yes</u>. / <u>No</u>. (Si lo has, explica por qué no lo escribiste en el formulario)

Q: Have you worked in the last five years?

A: <u>Yes</u>. / <u>No</u>.

Q: Are you currently employed? OR
                Do you have a job?
A: <u>Yes</u>. / <u>No</u>.

Q: Why aren't you working?
A: (¡Sé honrado!)

Q: What is your occupation? OR
                What do you do? OR
                What kind of work do you do?
A: I am / was a _____. OR <u>I am retired</u>.

Q: Where do you work? OR
                For whom do you work? OR
                Who is your employer? OR
                How do you support yourself?
A: I work at _____.

Q: How long have you worked there? OR
                How long have you held this job?
A: I have worked there for _____ years.

Q: Who was your employer before that?
A: _____.

Q: Please list your employers in the past five years.
A: I have worked for _____ (enumera
                toda tu historia de empleo).

Q: Is this list of employers complete?
A: <u>Yes</u>. / <u>No</u>. (si no, explica por qué no lo escribiste en el
                formulario).

Parte 7: Tiempo fuera de los Estados Unidos

Q: Since becoming a permanent resident, have you ever left
                the United States? OR
                Have you left the United States since you became a perma-
                nent resident? OR

Since coming to the United States, have you traveled to any other country? OR

Have you visited any other country since becoming a permanent resident?

A: <u>Yes</u>. / <u>No</u>.

Q: How many times have you left the United States since you became a permanent resident?

A: _____ times

Q: How long were you away?

A: I was gone for _____ <u>days</u> / <u>weeks</u> / <u>months</u> / <u>years</u>.

Q: Which country did you travel to? OR

Q: Where did you go?

A: I went to _____.

Q: Why did you leave the United States?

A: I left because _____.

Q: Did any of these trips last six months or more?

A: <u>Yes</u>. / <u>No</u>. (Si la respuesta es sí, está dispuesto a explicar por qué).

Q: When was your most recent trip? OR

Q: When was the last time you left the United States?

A: It was _____.

Q: For how long were you in _____ (país)?

A: I was there for _____ <u>days</u> / <u>weeks</u> / <u>months</u> / <u>years</u>.

Parte 8: Información sobre tu historia marital

Las siguientes preguntas tratan de tu estatus marital. Si nunca te has casado con nadie, no tienes que leer esta sección. Puedes resumir en la página 54.

Q: What is your marital status?

A: I am <u>single</u> / <u>married</u> / <u>divorced</u> / <u>widowed</u>.

Q: Have you ever been married?

A: <u>Yes</u>. / <u>No</u>.

Q: Are you married?
A: <u>Yes</u>. / <u>No</u>.

Q: How many times have you been married?
A: I have been married _____ times.

Q: What is the full name of your husband / wife?
A: My husband's / wife's name is _____.

Q: What is your husband's / wife's date of birth?
A: __ __ / __ __ / __ __ __ __

Q: When did you marry him / her?
A: __ __ / __ __ / __ __ __ __

Q: What is his / her current address?
A: _____.

Q: Is your wife / husband a U.S. citizen?
A: <u>Yes</u>. / <u>No</u>.

Q: What is his / her immigration status?
A: <u>He</u> / <u>she is a permanent resident</u>. OR
A: <u>He</u> / <u>she is a U.S. citizen</u>.

Q: What is his / her country of citizenship?
A: _____.

Q: When did he / she become a U.S. citizen?
A: __ __ / __ __ / __ __ __ __.

Q: If your husband / wife is NOT a U.S. citizen, what is his / her country of origin?
A: <u>He</u> / <u>she is from</u> _____.

Q: If your husband / wife is NOT a U.S. citizen, what is his / her USCIS A-number?
A: <u>His</u> / <u>her USCIS A number is</u> _____.

Q: Have you ever been divorced?
A: <u>Yes</u>. / <u>No</u>.

Q: Why did you get a divorce?

A: _____.

Parte 9: Información sobre tus hijos

Q: How many children do you have? OR

 How many sons and daughters do you have?

A: ____

Q: What are the full names of your sons and daughters?

A: (Di todos los nombres y apellidos de cada hijo.)

Q: Do your children live with you?

A: Yes. / No.

Q: How many people live in your house?

A: ____ people: myself, (Mi esposo/a), and ___ children.

Q: With whom do you live?

A: I live with _____.

Q: Where do your children live?

A: My children live with me in _____. OR other: _____.

Q: Did any of your children stay in your native country?

A: Yes. / No.

Q: When were your children born?

A: One was born in _____, one in _____, and one in _____. (o más)

Q: Were they all born in the United States?

A: Yes. / No.

Más preguntas

Todas las preguntas siguientes se contestan con "sí" o "no". Fíjate en cómo empieza cada pregunta; te sugiere la manera correcta de contestarla. Es necesario, sin embargo, que entiendas lo que significa cada pregunta.

MODELOS DE ORACIÓN

Para las oraciones que empiezan con:	Respuesta:
"Have you ever…"	No
"Did you ever …"	No
"Do you owe …"	No
"Do you believe …"	Yes
"Do you support …"	Yes
"If the law requires it, are you willing …"	Yes

Preguntas generales

Q: **Have you ever** claimed (in writing or in any other way) to be a U.S. citizen? OR
Have you ever pretended to be a U.S. citizen?

Q: **Have you ever** registered to vote in any federal, state, or local election in the United States? OR
Have you ever voted in any federal, state, or local election in the United States?

Q: Since becoming a lawful permanent resident, **have you ever** failed to file a required federal, state, or local tax return? OR
Do you owe any federal, state, or local taxes that are overdue?

Q: Do you have any title of nobility in any foreign country? OR
Were you born with or have you acquired any title of nobility? OR
Are you a king, queen, duke, earl, prince, or princess, or do you have any other title of nobility?

Q: **Have you ever** been declared legally incompetent or been confined to a mental institution within the last five years? OR

Have you ever been in a mental hospital? OR

Have you ever been confined as a patient in a mental institution?

A: <u>No</u>. (If yes, explain.)

Affiliations

Q: **Have you ever** been affiliated with any organization, association, fund, foundation, party, club, or society?

Q: **Have you ever** been a member of the Communist Party?

Q: **Have you ever** been a member of any other totalitarian party?

Q: **Have you ever** been a member of a terrorist organization?

Q: **Have you ever** advocated the overthrow of any government by force or violence?

Q: **Have you ever** persecuted any person because of race, religion, national origin, membership in a particular social group, or political opinion?

Q: **Have you ever** worked for or been associated with the Nazi government of Germany?

A: <u>No</u>. (If yes, explain why.)

Continuous Residence

Q: Have you ever called yourself a "nonresident" on a federal, state, or local tax return?

Q: Have you ever failed to file a federal, state, or local tax return because you considered yourself to be a nonresident?

A: <u>No</u>.

Paying Taxes

Q: **Have you ever** failed to file a federal income tax return?

Q: Was there ever a year when you didn't file your federal tax forms?

A: <u>No</u>. (If you have failed to file taxes, say "yes" and explain why.)

Q: Have you filed your federal taxes every year?

Q: Do you pay taxes?

A: <u>Yes</u>.

Military Service

Q: **Have you ever** served in the U.S. Armed Forces?

Q: **Have you ever** left the United States to avoid being drafted into the U.S. Armed Forces? OR
Have you ever left the United States so you didn't have to fight in a war?

Q: **Have you ever** applied for any kind of exemption from military service in the U.S. Armed Forces?

Q: **Have you ever** deserted from the U.S Armed Forces?

Q: **Have you ever** failed to comply with Selective Service laws?

Q: **Have you ever** tried to avoid military service?

A: <u>No</u>.

Removal, Exclusion, and Deportation Proceedings

Q: Are removal, exclusion, rescission, or deportation proceedings pending against you?

Q: **Have you ever** been removed, excluded, or deported from the United States?

Q: **Have you ever** been ordered to be removed, excluded, or deported from the United States?

Q: **Have you ever** applied for any kind of relief from removal, exclusion, or deportation?

A: <u>No</u>.

Criminal Record

Q: **Have you ever** committed a crime or offense for which you were not arrested?

Q: **Have you ever** been arrested, cited, or detained by any law enforcement officer?

Q: **Have you ever** been charged with committing any crime or offense?

Q: **Have you ever** been placed in an alternative sentencing or a rehabilitative program?

Q: **Have you ever** received a suspended sentence, been placed on probation, or been paroled?

Q: **Have you ever** been in jail or prison?

Q: **Have you ever** lied to any U.S. government official?

A: <u>No</u>. (If you have ever been arrested, say "yes," and explain why.)

Buen carácter moral

Estas preguntas tratan de tu carácter moral. En la mayoría de casos, la respuesta es "no", porque ten cuidado, que hay algunos ejemplos más complejos. Léelas con cuidado y aprende las definiciones de las palabras clave de la lista siguiente:

Q: Have you ever been a **habitual drunkard**? OR
Were you ever drunk every day?

A: <u>No</u>, I drink only a little. OR
<u>No</u>, I don't drink alcohol.

Q: Have you ever advocated or practiced **polygamy**? OR
Have you ever been married to more than one person at the same time?

A: <u>No</u>.

Q: Have you ever been a **prostitute**? OR
Have you ever sold your body for money?

A: <u>No</u>, I've never taken money for sex.

Q: Have you ever knowingly and for gain helped any alien to enter the United States illegally? OR
Have you ever smuggled anyone into the United States? OR
Have you ever accepted money for sneaking someone into the United States?

A: <u>No</u>, I have never helped anyone enter the United States illegally.

Q: Have you ever bought or sold illegal drugs? OR
Have you ever been a trafficker in illegal drugs? OR
Have you ever carried illegal drugs for someone else? OR
Have you ever been a trafficker in cocaine or crack? OR
Have you ever bought or sold marijuana or speed?

A: No, I have never bought or sold illegal drugs.

Q: Have you ever received income from illegal **gambling**? OR
Did you ever get money illegally from gambling? OR
Have you ever received money from illegal gambling? OR
Have you ever received money or other goods from illegal gambling?

A: No, I don't gamble.

No hay casi ninguna duda de que aparecerán estas seis preguntas finales en tu entrevista; son los requisitos para el Juramento de Fidelidad a los Estados Unidos. La respuesta a cada pregunta debe ser "sí" si quieres hacerte ciudadano; pero, hay que repetir, es importante que entiendas lo que significan de todos modos. Estudia las preguntas y el vocabulario, y después lee el Juramento entero. Si pasas la entrevista, el oficial te pedirá que leas el Juramento y que lo firmes.

Q: 1. Do you support the **Constitution** and form of government of the United States?
2. Do you understand the full **Oath of Allegiance** to the United States?
3. Are you willing to take the full Oath of Allegiance to the United States?
4. If the law requires it, are you willing to **bear arms** on behalf of the United States?
5. If the law requires it, are you willing to perform **noncombatant services** in the U.S. Armed Forces?
6. If the law requires it, are you willing to perform work of national importance under civilian direction?

A: Yes.

Oath of Allegiance

I hereby declare, on oath, that I absolutely and entirely renounce and abjure all allegiance and fidelity to any foreign prince, potentate, state, or sovereignty, of whom or which I have heretofore been a subject or citizen; that I will support and defend the Constitution and laws of the United States when required by law; that I will bear true faith and allegiance to the same; that I will bear arms on behalf of the United States when required by law; that I will perform noncombatant service in the Armed Forces of the United States when required by law; that I will perform work of national importance under civilian direction when required by law; and that I take this obligation freely, without any mental reservation or purpose of evasion; so help me God.

Evaluación de lengua y conocimiento

Durante la entrevista, tendrás que demostrar que puedes leer y escribir un inglés básico. El oficial querrá saber que puedes entender el idioma. También evaluará, por medio del examen escrito, tu conocimiento de la historia y cívica básicas de los Estados Unidos; tu punto de partida es la lista de 100 preguntas en el Capítulo 6.

100 preguntas

El entrevistador te hará **diez** la historia y la cívica. Para salir bien en el examen, tendrás que contestar correctamente unos **seis**. El Capítulo 6 contiene todo lo que necesitarás saber.

Dictado

Después de contestar diez preguntas, el entrevistador te leerá una oración y te pedirá que las escribas en una hoja. Es buena idea practicar con la lista siguiente. Un amigo o familiar debe leer la oración en voz alta, y tú la debes escribir con cuidado en la línea abajo.

1. I love living in the United States.

   _____

2. I study English.

   _____

3. I study citizenship.

   _____

4. I want to be a citizen.

   _____

5. I want to be an American.

   _____

6. I live in New York City.

   _____

7. I live with my big family.

   _____

8. The president lives in the White House.

   _____

9. I want to become an American citizen.

   _____

10. I want to be a citizen of the United States.

    _____

11. I want to live near my brother.

    _____

12. I drive to work every day.

    _____

13. His wife works at home.

    _____

14. She works very hard at her job.

    _____

15. Their children go to school every morning.

_____

16. My daughter likes her teacher.

_____

17. My sons want to go to college.

_____

18. My family is happy to be in America.

_____

19. We believe in freedom.

_____

20. I believe in the Constitution.

_____

21. I believe in freedom and the Constitution.

_____

22. America is the land of the brave.

_____

23. America is the home of the free.

_____

24. I have four children.

_____

25. I hope my children will be happy in America.

_____

26. I live with my children and my husband.

_____

27. We have a new home and we are a happy family.

_____

28. America is the land of freedom.

_____

29. Many people come to America for freedom.

_____

30. It is important for all citizens to vote.

_____

31. Congress passes laws in the United States.

_____

32. The American flag has stars and stripes.

_____

33. Citizens of the United States have the right to vote.

_____

34. The people have a voice in government.

_____

35. I want to be a citizen because I love America.

_____

36. The Statue of Liberty was a gift from France.

_____

37. Our government is divided into three branches.

_____

38. Congress meets in Washington, D.C.

_____

39. The president enforces the laws.

_____

40. George Washington was the first American president.

_____

41. The colors of the American flag are read, white, and blue.

_____

42. The stars of the American flag are white.

_____

43. The United States of America has 50 states.

_____

44. Only Congress can declare war.

_____

45. People vote for the president in November.

_____

46. I studied for my citizenship exam with a book.

_____

47. I studied for my citizenship exam on my own.

_____

48. I studied for my citizenship exam in a class.

_____

49. All students in my class will be taking a citizenship exam.

_____

50. I want to become an American so I can vote.

_____

Lectura

Ahora el entrevistador te mostrará una oración para que la leas en voz alta. Para practicar, lee la siguiente lista de oraciones. (Aparecen también en la página de Web USCIS en www.uscis.gov.)

Civics/History

A senator is elected for six years.

All people want to be free.

America is the land of freedom.

All U.S. citizens have the right to vote.

America is the home of the brave.

America is the land of the free.

Citizens have the right to vote.

Congress is part of the American government.

Congress meets in Washington, D.C.

Congress passes laws in the United States.

George Washington was the first president.

I want to be a citizen of the United States.

I want to be an American citizen.

I want to become an American so I can vote.

It is important for all citizens to vote.

Many people come to America for freedom.

Many people have died for freedom.

Martha Washington was the first First Lady.

Only Congress can declare war.

Our government is divided into three branches.

People in America have the right to freedom.

People vote for the president in November.

The American flag has stars and stripes.

The American flag has 13 stripes.

The capitol of the United States is in Washington, D.C.

The colors of the flag are red, white, and blue.

The Constitution is the supreme law of our land.

The flag of the United States has 50 stars.

The House and Senate are parts of Congress.

The people have a voice in government.

The people in the class took a citizenship test.

The president enforces the laws.

The president has the power of veto.

The president is elected every four years.

The president lives in the White House.

The president lives in Washington, D.C.

The president must be an American citizen.

The president must be born in the United States.

The president signs bills into law.

The stars of the American flag are white.

The Statue of Liberty was a gift from France.

The stripes of the American flag are red and white.

The White House is in Washington, D.C.

The United States of America has 50 states.

There are 50 states in the Union.

There are three branches of government.

Everyday Life

He came to live with his brother.

He has a very big dog.

She knows how to ride a bike.

He wanted to find a job.

She wanted to talk to her boss.

He went to the post office.

His wife is at work right now.

His wife worked in the house.

I am too busy to talk today.

I bought a blue car today.

I came to _____ (city) today for my interview.

I count the cars as they pass by the office.

I drive a blue car to work.

I go to work every day.

I have three children.

I know how to speak English.

I live in the state of _____.

I want to be a U.S. citizen.

It is a good job to start with.

My car does not work.

She can speak English very well.

She cooks for her friends.

She is my daughter, and he is my son.

He needs to buy some new clothes.

He wanted to live near his brother.

She was happy with her house.

The boy threw a ball.

The children bought a newspaper.

The children play at school.

The children wanted a television.

The man wanted to get a job.

The teacher was proud of her class.

The red house has a big tree.

They are a very happy family.

They are very happy with their car.

They buy many things at the store.

They came to live in the United States.

They go to the grocery store.

They have horses on their farm.

They live together in a big house.

They work well together.

Today, I am going to the store.

Today is a sunny day.

Warm clothing was on sale in the store.

We have a very clean house.

You cook very well.

You drink too much coffee.

You work very hard at your job.

Repaso

Ten presentes las frases útiles, y además está dispuesto a contestar todas las preguntas siguientes. Debes hacer un repaso de esta sección.

Frases útiles
- ◆ Please repeat that.
- ◆ Please speak more slowly.
- ◆ Please speak louder.

Saludos y conversación trivial
- ◆ How are you?
- ◆ What is the weather like today? / How is the weather?
- ◆ What did you have for breakfast this morning?
- ◆ How did you get here today? / Who came with you?
- ◆ What day of the week is today?
- ◆ Do you know why you are here today?
- ◆ Why do you want to be a U.S. citizen?
- ◆ Do you have any questions before we begin?
- ◆ Have you studied for the citizenship test? What did you do?

Preguntas sobre fechas
- ◆ When did you first come to the United States?
- ◆ How long have you been a permanent resident?
- ◆ When was your last trip out of the United States?
- ◆ How long were you gone?
- ◆ How long have you lived at (current address)?
- ◆ How long have you worked at (current job)?

Preguntas sobre lugares
- ◆ Where did you first enter the United States? / What is your port of entry?
- ◆ What is your country of nationality?
- ◆ What is your country of birth? / Where were you born?

Preguntas "¿has hecho alguna vez?"

- ◆ Have you ever failed to file a tax return?
- ◆ Have you ever been part of the Communist Party / a terrorist organization?
- ◆ Have you ever been arrested, indicted, or convicted of a crime?

Otro modo de categorizar estas preguntas es según la primera palabra. Escucha con cuidado la primera palabra y las palabras clave de cada pregunta. Si no las eschucas la primera vez, pide que el entrevistador repita la pregunta.

Preguntas "¿qué?"

- ◆ **What** is your name?
- ◆ **What** is your Social Security number?
- ◆ **What** is your home telephone number?
- ◆ **What** is your date of birth?
- ◆ **What** is your marital status?
- ◆ **What** is your nationality?
- ◆ **What** is your height / weight / eye color / hair color?
- ◆ **What** is your address?
- ◆ **What** is your wife's / husband's name?
- ◆ **What** is his / her immigration status?

Preguntas "¿cómo?"

- ◆ **How** are you?
- ◆ **How** is the weather?
- ◆ **How** did you get here?
- ◆ **How** do you spell your last name?

Preguntas "¿cuánto tiempo hace?"

- ◆ **How long** have you been a permanent resident?
- ◆ **How long** have you lived at (current address)?
- ◆ **How long** have you worked at (current job)?
- ◆ **How long** did the trip outside the United States last?
- ◆ **How long** have you been married?

Preguntas "¿dónde?"
- ◆ **Where** were you born?
- ◆ **Where** do you live?
- ◆ **Where** do you work?
- ◆ **Where** did you go (when you last left the United States)?
- ◆ **Where** were your children born?

Preguntas "¿cuándo?"
- ◆ **When** were you born?
- ◆ **When** did you come to the United States?
- ◆ **When** did you get your permanent resident card?
- ◆ **When** did you get married?
- ◆ **When** did your spouse become a citizen?
- ◆ **When** did you move to (current address)?
- ◆ **When** was your last trip outside the United States?
- ◆ **When** did you return?
- ◆ **When** were your children born?

Preguntas "por qué?"
- ◆ **Why** do you want to become a citizen?
- ◆ **Why** were you out of the country for six months or longer?
- ◆ **Why** did you get divorced?
- ◆ **Why** aren't you working?

Cuando termina el examen

En algunos casos el entrevistador te dirá que has tenido éxito en el momento que termina el examen. Son buenas noticias, por supuesto— sabrás que el proceso ha merecido todo el trabajo que has hecho. Entonces puedes concentrarte en la ceremonia de "*swearing-in*".

Por otra parte, si no sales bien en el examen, el entrevistador te sugerirá que lo tomes de nuevo. La ley federal decreta que te notifique dentro de 120 días si o no se acepta tu solicitud. Si te asigna una segunda fecha para tomar el examen y no vas ese día a la oficina, sin embargo, se rechazará la solicitud y tendrás que empezar el proceso entero de nuevo.

Una vez que se acepte tu solicitud, tu registro se actualiza en el sistema USCIS. Recibirás un certificado y una invitación a la ceremonia *swearing-in* para tomar el Juramento de Fidelidad. En algunos casos tiene lugar en un palacio de justicia; en otros se usa la oficina USCIS. Pase lo que pase, es oficial: ¡serás ciudadano!

Como ves, entonces, es muy importante estudiar y estar preparado el día del examen. Te hemos dado muchas preguntas ejemplares para estudiar a través de este capítulo. El capítulo siguiente te ofrece la lista completa y oficial de preguntas que usa USCIS. Lee estos dos capítulos con frecuencia mientras esperas la entrevista, y sobre todo, ¡respetas el horario que has hecho!

☆ ☆ ☆

LA HISTORIA DE SASHA

SALÍ DE Yugoslavia y llegué a los Estados Unidos a finales del año de 1991, durante los primeros pasos de la violencia que se desarrollaba en mi patria. Nací en la República de Serbia en una ciudad pequeña al lado de Hungría. A finales de los años 1980, cuando podría ser elegido para luchar en las fuerzas militares, era estudiante universitaria y no tenía que participar. Estudiaba informática y esperaba trabajar fuera de Yugoslavia. Fui a una feria profesional en Belgrado y pronto empecé a trabajar en las Filipinas por una compañía grande americana. Para mí esto fue estratégico porque quería vivir un día en los Estados Unidos.

Después de dos años me transfirieron a la oficina en Nueva York, donde trabajaba muchas horas, lograba un nivel más alto de inglés y me adaptaba a la vida americana. Conocí a muchos amigos nuevos, sobre todo europeos. Durante esta etapa también aprendí más de la tecnología, y así continuaba desarrollar mi carrera. Los abogados de la compañía me consiguieron una tarjeta verde y empezaron mi proceso de naturalización. Mi pasaporte serbio no se aceptaba en algunos países, y aunque tenía mucho orgullo de ser de Serbia, me di cuenta de que, para viajar sin problemas, habría de hacerme ciudadano estadounidense.

Hacerme ciudadano fue una decisión difícil. El paisaje americano fuera de Nueva York me parece lo serbio. A veces echo de menos mi patria; otras veces, sobre todo cuando leo periódicos y hay noticias malas, me alegro de no tener que vivir allí.

En medio del proceso de naturalización, otra compañía me ofreció trabajo que no podía rechazar. Desafortunadamente, retrasó el proceso: tenía que superar mucho "*red tape*", y mi compañía antigua se retrasaba en enviarme el papeleo requisito.

Porque trabajaba tanto, busqué a un abogado con especialidad en la inmigración para ayudarme con el resto del proceso. Incluso con su ayuda, pasó cuatro años antes de que completara la naturalización. El verano pasado, por fin tomé el examen de ciudadanía, que consistía en 20 preguntas casi indistinguibles. Fue muy buena decisión estudiar la sección de cívica; no me había preocupado del aspecto lingüístico, ya que hacía diez años que vivía en los Estados Unidos y hablaba inglés muy bien. Me sorprendió ver tanta gente en mi ceremonia en Nueva Jersey. Estoy contento: puedo visitar a mis amigos y mi familia, y puedo viajar libremente en otros países europeos como estadounidense.

Palabras claves

Esta lista consiste en términos importantes en el contexto de la naturalización, y sus definiciones. Estudia esta lista para aprender lo que significa cada palabra. Tal familiaridad te ayudará a salir bien en el examen.

Palabra	Lo que significa
A	
abolish	abolir; terminar absolutamente
address	dirección; donde vives
adopted	adoptado; puesto en efecto
advise	dar consejo a
affiliated	vinculado o conectado
alienage	el estatus de ser residente nacido en país extranjero
allies	aliados; amigos durante la guerra
amendments	cambios de un documento legal; enmienda
appointed	nombrado; elegido
arrested	arrestado; acusado por un policía
asylum	asilo; protección de ser deportado

B

banner	bandera
basic belief	creencia fundamental
bear arms	llevar armas
benefits	beneficios; ventajas
Bill of Rights	las primeras diez enmiendas que acompañan la Constitución; lista de derechos básicos
birthplace	lugar de nacimiento
born	nacido
branches	ramas; partes distintas

C

cabinet	grupo de 14 consejeros presidenciales
capital	ciudad donde está ubicado el gobierno
Capitol	edificio donde se reúne el Congreso
chief justice	juez principal de la Corte Suprema
citizen	ciudadano
citizenship	ciudadanía
civil rights leader	persona que ayuda a otra gente para lograr derechos
Civil War	guerra de 1861–1865 entre estados del norte y del sur
claimed	dijo como verdad
colonies	colonias; los 13 estados originales
Communist	persona que pertenece a un partido que apoya la redistribución de la propiedad
Congress	grupo que hace las leyes
conscientious objections	razones por no participar en una guerra
Constitution	la ley suprema del país
crime	crimen

D

Declaration of Independence	documento por medio del cual las colonias se liberaron de Inglaterra
Democracy	democracia; gobierno popular
democratic	democrático
democratic republic	la forma del gobierno estadounidense
deported	deportado
deserted	salió de las fuerzas armadas sin permiso
different	diferente; otro
drafted	elegido en la llamada de filas

E

Electoral College	grupo que oficialmente elige al presidente
Emancipation Proclamation	documento según el cual se liberaron los esclavos

employer	patrono
enemies	enemigos (en una guerra)
executive branch	rama ejecutiva: presidente, vicepresidente y Cabinet
exemption	exención
explain	explicar; dar información detallada

F, G, H

false testimony	mentir en un juicio
gamble	apostar a algo
governor	líder de un estado
head executive	líder más alto; presidente
habitual drunkard	borracho habitual

I

illegal	ilegal; contra la ley
inaugurated	investido
income tax	impuesto sobre la renta
incompetent	incapaz
independence	independencia
Independence Day	el 4 de julio
interpret	interpretar
introduction	introducción

J, L

job	trabajo; empleo
judicial branch	rama judicial; sistema de cortes
legislative branch	rama legislativa; Congreso
liberty	libertad

M

maiden name	nombre de soltera
marital status	estado civil
mayor	alcalde
mental institution	hospital para gente que padece de problemas psiquiátricos
mínimum	mínimo

N

national anthem	himno nacional
national importance	de alta importancia para los Estados Unidos
Native Americans	nativos; indios; gente que vivía en América cuando llegaron los peregrinos
natural-born citizen	persona autóctona
noncombatant service	ayudar al militar sin luchar

O

oath	juramento
Oath of Allegiance	juramento de fidelidad a los Estados Unidos
occupation	tipo de empleo

P

passport	pasaporte; documento oficial que te permite que viajes libremente
persecution	persecución; maltratamiento por razones de raza, religión, nacionalidad o política
Pilgrims	peregrinos; gente que fue a América en un barco que se llamaba el Mayflower
political party	partido político
polygamy	poligamia; estar casado con más de una persona al mismo tiempo
port of entry	donde una persona entra en un país
Preamble	la introducción a la Constitución
prostitute	prostituto/a

R

reelected	elegido de nuevo
registered	registrado oficialmente
represent	representar; actuar por parte de algo
representatives	representantes en el House of Representatives
Revolutionary War	guerra revolucionaria contra Inglaterra, 1776–1783

S

senators	senadores; oficiales en el Senate
slave	esclavo
smuggle	pasar de contrabando
Supreme Court	corte más alta de los Estados Unidos

T

term	período de servicio público
tried	juzgado en una corte

U, W

union	los Estados Unidos
united	unidos
warrant	mandamiento judicial
White House	casa blanca; donde vive el presidente en Washington, D.C.

Historia y cívica estadounidenses

EN TU ENTREVISTA, el oficial de USCIS te hará preguntas específicas sobre la historia y cívica estadounidenses. El Capítulo 6 contiene la lista oficial, en inglés. Para tener más confianza durante el examen oral, en todo caso, es bueno entender el *contexto* de las preguntas relevantes. En este capítulo, te damos un resumen de las áreas de la historia estadounidense que incluye el examen. Leer la historia de los Estados Unidos es una manera excelente de aumentar tu preparación. Puedes memorizar datos y nada más si prefieres, pero esperamos que leas este capítulo más narrativo—aprenderás cosas interesantes acerca de tu nuevo país. Y hemos añadido varias tipos de información que te ayudará mientras estudias la historia de nuestro país—del descubrimiento de las Américas a la Guerra Civil. Incluimos, después, datos básicos y necesarios sobre el gobierno estadounidense.

☆ **CONTEXT:** las circunstancias en que un suceso transcurre

Presidentes clave

Todos nuestros presidentes son importantes de algún modo, pero en el examen es más probable que aparezcan estos cuatro:

◆ El primer presidente de los Estados Unidos fue George Washington.

◆ El presidente que escribió la Declaración de Independencia fue Thomas Jefferson.

◆ El presidente que terminó el sistema de esclavitud africana fue Abraham Lincoln.

◆ El presidente actual es George W. Bush (a principios del año de 2008, cuando se publicó este libro).

Pasó el año . . .

1492   **El Nuevo Mundo**
Cristóbal Colón descubre América.

1500–1700   **La Edad de Exploración**
Varias exploradores navegan al Nuevo Mundo y se instalan en las regiones que hoy actualmente son las Américas del Norte, Central y del Sur.

1620   **Peregrinos**
Un grupo inglés sale de Inglaterra en un barco que se llama el *Mayflower* por razones de libertad religiosa. Llegan a Plymouth Rock en Massachusetts. La historia de los Estados Unidos empieza.

Mayflower Compact

Los peregrinos escribieron un documento para dar un esbozo del gobierno del Nuevo Mundo. La Constitución estadounidense se basa en los principios que se expresan en este documento.

Thanksgiving/Día de accíon de gracias

Después de una cosecha muy exitosa basada en el método nativo de cultivar la tierra, se celebra el primer *Día de accíon de gracias*.

1660–1776 Colonias británicas en América

Fue el rey inglés el que gobernaba las colonias. La vida económica de las colonias dependía de Inglaterra, y a los ingleses también les gustaba la existencia de un mercado ensanchado. Durante esta etapa, más gente cruzó el Océano Atlántico de Inglaterra; también vinieron grupos de Irlanda, Francia, Holanda, Alemania y España. Creció la población y se organizaron 13 colonias distintas, administradas por el rey inglés. En las colonias del Norte había granjas pequeñas, comercio y unas fábricas. En las colonias del Sur, debido a tierras más extensas y un clima más caliente, se desarrollaba agricultura de un nivel más alto. Se formaron plantaciones que especializaron en *"cash crops"*–tabaco, azúcar y algodón.

1740 Empieza la esclavitud

Para mantener las grandes plantaciones en las colonias del Sur, se importaron esclavos de África.

1754–1763 Guerra de Siete Años

Los franceses, con la ayuda de los indios (a quienes tampoco les gustaba la presencia británica), lucharon contra los ingleses en América.

1763–1775 Impuestos sin representación

Los ingleses imponían impuestos graves, y el gobierno imperial al mismo tiempo empezó a interferir en la vida cotidiana de los colonos. **Patrick Henry**, un colono bien franco, se opuso a los impuestos, sobre todo el **Stamp Act** de 1765. Hizo un discurso famoso que terminó con la frase **"Give me liberty or give me death"** ("Que me den la muerte si no la libertad"). Se reunieron representantes de las 13 colonias en Filadelfia para discutir sus problemas con el gobierno inglés. Esta reunión se llama el **First Continental Congress** (primer congreso continental) de septiembre del año de 1774. Los representantes redactaron un documento llamado la **Declaration of Rights** (declaración de derechos) y lo enviaron a King George II (Rey Jorge Segundo) de Inglaterra. Pidieron cambios específicos por lo que se refería al tratamiento de los colonos. Querían más libertad, menos impuestos y más representación política.

1775 "The Shot Heard 'Round the World" "El disparo que se oye por todo el mundo"

En la región de Boston, sucedieron varias eventos famosos. En el **Boston Tea Party** ("reunión bostoño para tomar el té"), los colonos tiraron grandes cantidades de té inglés (una cosa bajo muchos impuestos) en el mar en Boston Harbor. Representó su frustración con impuestos. Inventaron un eslogan: "No taxation without representation", que enfadó a los ingleses. Los soldados británicos empezaron a fusilar a los colonos. **Paul Revere**, a caballo, avisó a la población de Boston, gritando "¡Vienen los ingleses! ¡Vienen los ingleses!" Los colonos resistieron el poder absoluto de la corona inglesa, y varios enemigos de Inglaterra—sobre todo Francia—ayudaron a las colonias. Así empezó la **Guerra Revolucionaria**.

1776 La Declaración de Independencia

El Segundo Congreso Continental se reunió en Filadelfia el 4 de julio de 1776. Durante esta reunión, los representantes de las 13 colonias redactaron la Declaración de Independencia, escrita por Thomas Jefferson, y eligieron a George Washington como comandante de las Fuerzas Armadas Continentales. Las colonias cambiaron de nombre: se hicieron los "Estados Unidos de América".

1776–1783 ## Los Artículos de Confederación

Los representantes decidieron que sería necesario algún tipo de documento para estructurar el gobierno nuevo. Redactaron los *Articles of Confederation* (Artículos de Confederacíon), un esbozo temporario de los principios básicos del gobierno estadounidense. Funcionaría más o menos bien hasta que se escribiera la Constitución.

La Constitución

Después de la Guerra Revolucionaria, los 13 estados se dieron cuenta de que los Artículos de Confederación no constituían una forma bastante estricta de gobierno. El gobierno federal, según ellos, no tenía casi ningún poder ni la habilidad de organizar el sistema de impuestos. Volvieron los representantes a Filadelfia y redactaron la Constitución de los Estados Unidos. Cada estado tendría que ratificar el documento—es decir, estar de acuerdo con las nuevas reglas—y se pasó unánimemente el año de 1789.

1789–1860 ## La Gran Expansión

Durante estos años la población estadounidense creció y se distribuyó por la parte oeste del continente. Fue una época próspera. En el Norte, se abolió la esclavitud, mientras que se conservaba en el Sur. Esta cuestión y otras dividieron la nación.

1861–1865 ## La Guerra Civil

La "guerra entre los estados" fue un conflicto sangriento, el más violento que había transcurrido en tierras americanas. Resultó en más muertes individuales que ninguna guerra antes ni después.

1865 ## Termina la esclavitud

El presidente Abraham Lincoln, a través de la *Emancipation Proclamation*, eliminó el sistema de esclavitud; todos los esclavos se liberaron. En abril de 1865, una persona lo fusiló y mató.

☆

El día de accíon gracias

El día de fiesta que se observa el cuarto día jueves del mes de noviembre representa la primera cosecha que compartieron los peregrinos con los indios en el Nuevo Mundo. Los colonos se sentían agradecidos por la comida abundante, la paz y la libertad que tenían al vivir en esta tierra. El día de fiesta se sirve pavo porque hay pavos en Norteamérica. También se sirven maíz y arándanos—vegetales y frutas que los peregrinos descubrieron por primera vez en el Nuevo Mundo.

Las 13 colonias originales

Massachusetts

New Hampshire

Rhode Island

Connecticut

New York

New Jersey

Pennsylvania

Delaware

Maryland

Virginia

North Carolina

South Carolina

Georgia

¿Sabes que . . .

... las primeras reglas que se referían a ciudadanía estadounidense se establecieron en un Acto del 26 de marzo de 1790? La primera ley federal de naturalización fijó dos principios fundamentales que persiguen hoy día en nuestro código legal: el requisito de haber sido residente de los Estados Unidos por un período mínimo, y el de haber demostrado un buen carácter moral.

La Constitución de los Estados Unidos

La Constitución, cuando se escribió, tomó medidas para establecer un fuerte gobierno nacional de tres ramas: legislativa, judicial y ejecutiva.

Las tres ramas del gobierno

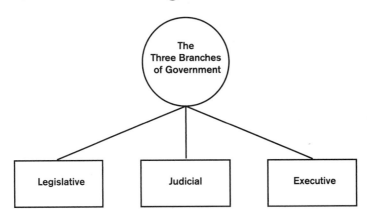

Rama legislativa

➤ La rama legislativa del gobierno se llama *Congress* (el Congreso).

➤ El Congreso hace las leyes de los Estados Unidos.

➤ El Congreso consiste en dos partes: el *Senado* y la Casa de Representantes.

➤ Los miembros del Congreso son elegidos por ciudadanos adultos de los Estados Unidos.

➤ El Congreso se reúne en el Capitol en Washington, D.C.

➤ Hay 100 senadores en el Congreso—dos de cada estado.

➤ El mandato de un senador es de seis años.

➤ No se limita el número de mandatos consecutivos.

➤ Hay 435 miembros de la Casa de Representantes. El número de representantes para cada estado se basa en la población de ese estado.

➤ Cada representante se elige por un mandato de dos años.

➤ No se limita el número de mandatos consecutivos.

Rama judicial

➤ La Corte Suprema es la rama judicial de nuestro gobierno.

➤ El deber de la Corte Suprema es interpretar las leyes y la Constitución.

➤ El juez principal de la Corte Suprema es John G. Roberts.

➤ El presidente elige los jueces, y el Congreso tiene que confirmar sus selecciones.

➤ Hay nueve jueces de la Corte Suprema.

➤ La Corte Suprema es la corte más alta y poderosa de los Estados Unidos.

Rama ejecutiva

➤ La rama ejecutiva consiste en el presidente, el vicepresidente y los miembros del Cabinet.

➤ El presidente de los Estados Unidos se elige por un mandato de cuatro años.

➤ Si muere el presidente, el vicepresidente se hace presidente.

➤ Hay un límite al número de mandatos: un presidente no puede ganar más que dos. Para hacerse presidente, es necesario que un candidato tenga el apoyo del Electoral College—no exclusivamente la mayoría de votantes.

➤ El *Speaker* de la Casa de Representantes se hace presidente si mueren el presidente y el vicepresidente.

➤ Para estar elegible como candidato para la presidencia, es necesario haber nacido en los Estados, tener al menos 35 años y haber vivido en los Estados Unidos al menos 14 años.

➤ El presidente vive en la Casa Blanca: 1600 Pennsylvania Ave., Washington, D.C.

➤ El ejecutivo principal de un estado es el *governor*—el gobernador.

➤ El ejecutivo principal de una ciudad es el *mayor*—el alcalde.

Datos sobre la Constitución

1. La Constitución es la ley suprema de los Estados Unidos de América.
2. Fue escrito en el año de 1787.
3. Sólo se puede cambiar por medio de un acto del Congreso. Los cambios se llaman enmiendas, "amendments".
4. Hay 27 enmiendas.
5. Las diez primeras se llaman, juntamente, el *Bill of Rights*.
6. La introducción a la Constitución se llama el preámbulo.
7. Ciertos derechos y libertades que establece el *Bill of Rights* son:
   ◆ La libertad de expresión, prensa y religión.
   ◆ El derecho de todo ciudadano de más de 18 años de edad de votar, y el derecho de llevar armas.
   ◆ El gobierno no puede instalar a soldados en las casas privadas, y no puede hacer un registro sin mandamiento oficial.
   ◆ Una persona puede ser juzgada más de una vez por un crimen único, y un acusado tiene el derecho de la ayuda de un abogado.
   ◆ Todo ciudadano está protegido contra multas injustas y castigos crueles.

La bandera americana

   ◆ Los colores de la bandera son rojo, blanco y azul.
   ◆ Hay 50 estrellas blancas sobre un fondo azul, y representan los 50 estados.
   ◆ Hay 13 rayas rojas y blancas, y representan las colonias originales.

Conoce a tu estado

1. ¿Cuál es la capital de tu estado? _____
2. ¿Quién es el gobernador de tu estado? _____
3. ¿Quién es el alcalde de tu ciudad o pueblo? _____

Los Estados Unidos actuales

◆ La capital de los Estados Unidos es Washington, D.C.

◆ Los Estados Unidos es una república democrática.

El himno nacional de los Estados Unidos de América
The Star Spangled Banner
por Francis Scott Key, 1814

Oh say can you see, by the dawn's early light,
What so proudly we hail'd at the twilight's last gleaming?
Whose broad stripes and bright stars, thro' the perilous fight,
O'er the ramparts we watch'd were so gallantly streaming?
And the rocket's red glare, the bombs bursting in air,
Gave proof thro' the night that our flag was still there.
O say, does that Star Spangled Banner yet wave
O'er the land of the free and the home of the brave?

On the shore dimly seen throughout the mists of the deep
Where the foe's haughty host in dread silence reposes
What is that which the breeze o'er the towering steep
As it fitfully blows, half conceals, half discloses?
Now it catches the gleam of the morning's first beam
In full glory reflected now shrines on the stream.
'Tis the Star Spangled Banner, Oh long may it wave
O'er the land of the free and the home of the brave.

And where is that band who so hauntingly swore
That the havoc of war and the battle's confusion
A home and country, shall leave us no more?
Their blood was washed out their foul foot steps pollution
No refuge could save the hireling and slave
From the terror of flight or the gloom of the grave.
And the Star Spangled Banner in triumph doth wave
O'er the land of the free and the home of the brave.

Oh thus be it e'er when free men shall stand
Between their lov'd homes and war's desolation!
Blest with vict'ry and peace, may the heav'n rescued land

Praise the Pow'r that has made and preserv'd us as a nation
And conquer we must when our cause is just
And this be our motto: "In God is our trust."
And the Star Spangled banner in triumph shall wave
O'er the land of the free and the home of the brave.

Lectura suplementaria

Como ciudadano estadounidense, es importante entender la historia de nuestra gran nación. Los diez libros que se enumeran abajo no sólo aumentarán tus estudios, sino también te darán un conocimiento bien ancho de la historia y un mejor concepto de cómo funciona este país. Cada libro tiene sus propias ventajas; todos son interesantes y bastante fáciles de leer. Cuando tienes tiempo libre, mira en la biblioteca o librería más cercana para determinar lo que te es más apropiado.

Twenty-Five Lessons in Citizenship, by D.L. Hennessey and Lenore Hennessey Richardson (D.L. Hennessey, 1997).

Voices of Freedom: English and Civics for the U.S. Citizenship Exam, by Bill Bliss with Steven J. Molinsky (Simon & Schuster, 1993).

Making Patriots, by Walter Berns (University of Chicago Press, 2001).

"To the Best of My Ability": The American Presidents, edited by James M. McPherson and David Rubel (Dorling Kindersley, 2000).

A People's History of the United States: 1492–Present, by Howard Zinn (HarperTrade, 1995).

Witness to America: An Illustrated Documentary History of the United States from the Revolution to Today (includes audio CD), edited by Stephen E. Ambrose (HarperCollins, 1999).

The Limits of Liberty: American History, 1607–1992. by Maldwyn Allen Jones (Oxford University Press, 1995).

The Great Republic: A History of the United States, by Winston S. Churchill (Random House, 1999).

What Every American Should Know about American History: 200 Events That Shaped the Nation, by Alan Axelrod and Charles Phillips (Adams, 1993).

The American Flag, by Patricia Ryon Quiri (Children's Press, 1998).

Aprender en línea

El Internet puede ser un recurso inestimable. Aquí tienes una lista de sitios que pueden aumentar tu programa de estudios. Si tienes una pregunta concreta o quieres aprender más sobre un tema, sólo has de buscar un sitio. (Estos sitios funcionaban cuando se publicó este libro. No podemos garantizar que todavía funcionen cuando estés leyendo este libro.)

History Channel Online
www.history.com

U.S.A. History.com
www.usahistory.com

Encyclopedia Britannica Online
www.Britannica.com

History.org
www.usahistory.org

Great Books Online
www.bartleby.com

50 States and Capitals
www.50states.com

The White House Homepage
www.whitehouse.gov

Grolier Online's The American Presidency
http://ap.grolier.com

American Memory: Historical Collections for the National Digital Library
http://memory.loc.gov

Preguntas oficiales USCIS y respuestas ejemplares

AQUÍ ENCUENTRAS UNA lista, organizada por categoría temática, de todas las preguntas oficiales de USCIS sobre la historia y cívica estadounidenses. Para salir bien en el examen, tendrás que saber las respuestas a muchas de estas preguntas. Para estudiar, se recomienda que tapes la columna de respuestas—o que estudies con un amigo que te lea las preguntas en voz alta. Si necesitas más ayuda aún, regresa al Capítulo 5 para la lección básica de cívica estadounidense.

Flashcards

Una idea divertida y efectiva para estudiar: hacer tarjetas con las preguntas oficiales USCIS. Sólo has de comprar fichas en una tienda; para cada ficha, escribe la pregunta en una cara y la respuesta correcta en la otra. ¡Con estas fichas te puedes examinar tú mismo!

La estructura del gobierno

1. How many branches are there in the government?

1. *three (3)*

2. What are the three branches of our government?

2. *executive, legislative, and judicial*

La rama legislativa

3. What is the legislative branch of our government?

3. *Congress*

4. Who makes the laws in the United States?

4. *Congress*

5. What is Congress?

5. *the Senate and House of Representatives*

6. What are the duties of Congress?

6. *to make laws*

7. Who elects the members of Congress?

7. *the voting citizens of the United States*

8. Where does Congress meet?

8. *the capitol in Washington, D.C.*

9. How many senators are there in Congress?

9. *one hundred (100)*

10. Why are there 100 senators in Congress?

10. *There are two (2) senators from each of the 50 states.*

11. Who are the two senators from your state?

11. *Each state has a different answer. Find out who are the two senators from your state.*

12. How long is an elected elected senator's term?

12. *six (6) years for each term he or she is elected*

13. How many times can a senator be re-elected?

13. *There is no limit.*

14. How many representatives are there in Congress?

14. *435 (four hundred thirty-five)*

15. How long is an elected representative's term?

15. *two (2) years for each term he or she is elected*

16. How many times can a representative be re-elected?

16. *There is no limit.*

La rama judicial

17. What is the judicial branch of our government?

17. *the Supreme Court*

18. What are the duties of the Supreme Court?

18. *to interpret laws and the Constitution*

19. Who is the chief justice of the Supreme Court?

19. *John Roberts*

20. Who selects the Supreme Court justices?

20. *the president*

21. How many Supreme Court justices are there?

21. *nine (9)*

22. What is the highest court in the United States?

22. *the Supreme Court*

La rama ejecutiva

23. What is the executive branch of our government?

23. *the president, vice president, and cabinet*

24. Who was the first president of the United States?

24. *George Washington*

25. Who is the president of the United States today?

25. *George W. Bush*

26. Who is the vice president today?

26. *Dick Cheney*

27. Who elects the president of the United States?

27. *the Electoral College*

28. How long is an elected president's term?

28. *four (4) years*

29. Who becomes president of the United States if the president should die?

29. *the vice president*

30. How many terms can a president serve?

30. *a maximum of two (2) terms*

31. Who becomes president of the United States if the president and vice president should die?

31. *the Speaker of the House of Representatives*

32. What are the requirements to be president?

32. *The president must be a natural-born citizen of the United States, at least thirty-five (35) years old, and have lived in the U.S. for at least fourteen (14) years.*

33. What special group advises the president?

33. *the cabinet*

34. What is the White House?

34. *the president's official home*

35. Where is the White House located?

35. *1600 Pennsylvania Avenue, Washington, D.C.*

36. In what month do we vote for the president?

36. *November*

37. In what month is the new president inaugurated?

37. *January*

38. What is the head executive of a state government called?

38. *governor*

39. What is the head executive of a city government called?

39. *mayor*

40. Who signs a bill into law?

40. *the president*

41. What is the name of the president's official home?

41. *the White House*

42. Who is commander in chief of the U.S. military?

42. *the president*

43. Who has the power to declare war?

43. *Congress*

La Constitución

44. What is the Constitution?

44. *the supreme law of the land*

45. Can the Constitution be changed?

45. *yes*

46. What do we call changes made to the Constitution?

46. *amendments*

47. How many amendments are there?

47. *twenty-seven (27)*

48. What is the supreme law of the United States?

48. *the Constitution*

49. What year was the Constitution written?

49. *1787*

50. What is the Bill of Rights?

50. *the first ten (10) amendments*

51. Where does freedom of speech come from?

51. *the Bill of Rights*

52. Whose rights are guaranteed by the Constitution and the Bill of Rights?

52. *everyone in America, including noncitizens*

53. What is the introduction to the Constitution called?

53. *the Preamble*

54. What are the first ten amendments to the Constitution called?

54. *the Bill of Rights*

55. Name three rights or freedoms guaranteed by the Bill of Rights.

55. *1. the freedoms of speech, press, and religion*
2. the right to bear arms
3. Government may not put soldiers in people's homes.
4. Government may not search or take a person's property without a warrant.
5. A person may not be tried for the same crime twice.

6. *A person charged with a crime has rights, including the right to a trial and a lawyer.*

7. *People are protected from unreasonable fines or cruel punishment.*

56. Name one right guaranteed by the First Amendment.

56. *freedom of speech, press, religion, peaceable assembly, and requesting change of government*

57. What is the most important right granted to U.S. citizens?

57. *the right to vote*

58. What is the minimum voting age in the United States?

58. *eighteen (18) years old*

¿Sabes que . . .

... unas 898.315 personas se naturalizaron y tomaron el Juramento de Fidelidad en el año de 2000?

Historia estadounidense

59. What is the 4th of July?

59. *Independence Day*

60. On what date was the Declaration of Independence adopted?

60. *July 4, 1776*

61. What is the basic belief stated in the Declaration of Independence?

61. *All men are created equal.*

62. Who was the main writer of the Declaration of Independence?

62. *Thomas Jefferson*

63. What is the date of Independence Day?

63. *July 4*

64. Which president was the first commander in chief of the U.S. military?

64. *George Washington*

65. What country did the United States gain its independence from?

65. *England*

66. What country did we fight during the Revolutionary War?

66. *England*

67. Who said, "Give me liberty or give me death"?

67. *Patrick Henry*

68. Which president is called the "father of our country"?

68. *George Washington*

69. Why did the pilgrims come to America?

69. *They were seeking religious freedom.*

70. Who helped the pilgrims in America?

70. *The Native Americans helped the pilgrims.*

71. What ship brought the pilgrims to America?

71. *the Mayflower*

72. What holiday was celebrated for the first time by the American colonists?

72. *Thanksgiving*

73. What were the original 13 states called?

73. *The original 13 states were called colonies.*

74. Can you name the original 13 states?

74. *Connecticut, New Hampshire, New York, New Jersey, Massachusetts, Pennsylvania, Delaware, Virginia, North Carolina, South Carolina, Georgia, Rhode Island, and Maryland*

75. Who wrote "The Star-Spangled Banner"?

75. *Francis Scott Key*

76. What is the national anthem of the United States?

76. *"The Star-Spangled Banner"*

77. Who was the president during the Civil War?

77. *Abraham Lincoln*

78. What did the Emancipation Proclamation do?

78. *The Emancipation Proclamation freed all slaves in the United States.*

79. Which president freed the slaves?

79. *Abraham Lincoln*

80. What are the 49th and 50th states of the Union?

80. *Alaska and Hawaii*

81. Who were America's enemies in World War II?

81. *Germany, Japan, and Italy*

82. Who was Martin Luther King, Jr.?

82. *a civil rights leader in the 1960s*

La bandera

83. What are the colors of our flag?

83. *red, white, and blue*

84. How many stars are on our flag?

84. *There are fifty (50) stars.*

85. What color are the stars on our flag?

85. *The stars are white.*

86. What do the stars on the flag represent?

86. *the fifty (50) states. There is one star for each state in the Union.*

87. How many stripes are on the flag?

87. *thirteen (13)*

88. What color are the stripes on the flag?

88. *The stripes are red and white.*

89. What do the stripes on the flag represent?

89. *the original thirteen (13) colonies*

Tu gobierno estatal

90. What is the capital of your state?

90. *Each state has a different answer. Find out the name of the capital of your state.*

91. Who is the current governor of your state?

91. *Each state has a different answer. Find out who is the governor of your state.*

92. Who is the head of your local government?

92. *Find out the name of your local mayor.*

Los Estados Unidos actuales

93. How many states are there in the United States?

93. *There are fifty (50) states.*

94. Name one purpose of the United Nations.

94. *for countries to talk about world problems and try to solve them peaceably*

95. Name one benefit of becoming a citizen of the United States.

95. *the right to vote, the right to travel with a U.S. passport, the right to serve on a jury, the right to apply for federal jobs*

96. What are the two major political parties in the United States today?

96. *the Democrat and Republican parties*

97. What kind of government does the United States have?

97. *a democratic republic*

98. What is the United States capitol?

98. *the place where Congress meets*

99. Where is the capital of the United States?

99. *Washington, D.C.*

100. What USCIS form is used to apply to become a naturalized citizen?

100. *Form N-400, the "Application to File Petition for Naturalization"*

Las diez áreas metropolitanas más comunes como destino de inmigrantes

En el año de 2003, el número más grande de inmigrantes intentaba vivir en las siguientes áreas:

Nueva York, Nueva York
Los Angeles/Long Beach, California
Chicago, Illinois

Washington, D.C. (área metropolitana)

Miami, Florida

Houston, Texas

Orange County, California

Oakland, California

Boston, Massachusetts

San José, California

¿Sabes que . . .

. . . Si tienes acceso al Internet, se puede imprimir *flash cards* USCIS de cívica, o escuchar las preguntas leídas en voz alta, en www.uscis.gov/files/nativedocuments/M-623.pdf?

☆ ☆ ☆

LA HISTORIA DE JULIO DOMÍNGUEZ, ESPECIALISTA LEGAL EN INMIGRACIÓN

Varios sucesos de mi juventud me inspiraron a hacerme abogado. Nací en Bakersfield, California, un ratito después que mis padres emigraron de México, D.F. Creciendo en una comunidad mayoritariamente hispánica en el Sur de California, los temas de inmigración y ciudadanía se discutían casi perpetuamente entre mi familia y grupo de amigos. Me parecía que a la comunidad le faltaba un buen abogado para ayudar a la gente trabajadora que quería ser ciudadanos. Me parecía (y lo vi personalmente cuando mi padre se naturalizó) que muchos especialistas, así llamados, de inmigración eran abogados estereotípicos con más interés en aprovecharse de la gente que en ayudarla. Al llegar a la facultad de derecho, hice un curso sobre la inmigración y la ley, y trabajé como voluntario en un programa para inmigrantes. Ayudando a gente de todas partes del mundo, se me hacía obvio que quería especializarme en la inmigración.

Hace casi diez años que ejerzo la profesión de abogado—de esos, nueve con la ley inmigratoria. Trabajo en una firma pequeña. Así sobrevivo económicamente. Cuando tengo tiempo libre, quiero regresar a mi comunidad para trabajar en casos privados—la mayoría de mis clientes son mexicanos, y muchas veces sin cobrarles nada—ayudando a gente trabajadora como mis padres. Es todo el pagamiento que puedo pedir. El proceso de naturalización es, en realidad, muy simple si entiendes lo que has de hacer.

He observado con todos mis clientes, corporativos y privados, que los requisitos de "presencia física" y de *Selective Service* son los más confusos. En estas áreas puede ser muy útil conocer a alguien que entienda los detalles legales. Hay muchos aspectos del proceso de naturalización que desaniman a candidatos, pero espero que todo el mundo se dé cuenta de que hay en toda comunidad varias personas como mi—personas que quieren ayudar a otra gente porque entendemos precisamente sus circunstancias.

Casos especiales

¿HAS ESCUCHADO ALGUNA vez a alguien que dice que para cada regla hay una excepción? En el Capítulo 2 has leído acerca de varias excepciones por lo que se refiere al examen oral. Las reglas se modifican un poco según el estatus del solicitante—por ejemplo estar casado con un ciudadano, o ser un soldado. En este capítulo leerás acerca de otros casos especiales que podrían afectar tu proceso de naturalización.

Mantener la calma en tus interacciones con USCIS

Unos consejos que tener presentes cuando llamas al USCIS o estás en la oficina pidiendo información:

➤ <u>Sé persistente</u>—Si el oficial que buscas no está, llámalo otra vez o pide a otra persona que pueda ayudarte. Si estás en la oficina, pide asistencia de toda forma que se pueda ofrecer.

➤ Mantente paciente—Es difícil entender lo que dice otra persona si estás enfadado (¡incluso si el inglés es tu lengua habitual!). Manten la mesura mientras escuchas.

➤ Sé cortés—Los representantes te ayudarán más efectivamente si te comportas de manera profesional y resignada.

➤ Repite tu pregunta—hasta que esté clara a todo el mundo.

➤ Repite la respuesta oficial USCIS—hasta que la entiendas.

➤ Sé paciente—No te hagas frustrado; ¡pronto serás ciudadano!

Sobre prometidos y el matrimonio

Un caso especial ocurre cuando un ciudadano quiere casarse con un no ciudadano. Aquí tienes unos pasos que seguir si te aplica (pero visita la página de Web de USCIS para averiguar si están correctos).

Un ciudadano de otro país que quiere ir a los Estados Unidos, casarse con un ciudadano estadounidense y vivir en los Estados Unidos tendrá que obtener una visa K-1. Para más información (ya que este libro trata de ciudadanía), envías un correo electrónico a usvisa@uscis.gov.

Para establecer elegibilidad para una visa K-1, también se necesita un formulario I-129F, *Petition for Alien Fiancé(e)*. Estos formularios no se pueden presentar si estás en otro país; sólo USCIS en los Estados Unidos los pueden aceptar. La oficina consular donde el prometido extranjero solicita su visa será notificado si la solicitud se acepta, y entonces le dará la visa K-1. Una solicitud está válida por los cuatro meses después de la fecha de acción USCIS, pero puede ser revalidado por un oficial consular. Es necesario que la boda tenga lugar dentro de los 90 días después de la llegada del prometido extranjero.

Inelegibilidad de visas

Aviso: Es posible que no recibas una visa si tienes una aflicción contagiosa; si padeces de un desorden peligroso físico o mental; si abusas drogas; si tienes una historia criminal que incluya prostitución o drogas; si has defraudado el gobierno para entrar en los Estados Unidos; o si estás inelegible para la ciudadanía.

Solicitar una visa de prometido

Se requieren, normalmente, estos documentos:

◆ Pasaporte válido
◆ Certificado de nacimiento
◆ Certificado de muerte de todos los esposos/as antiguos/as
◆ Certificado policial de todo lugar en que has vivido más de seis meses desde 16 años de edad
◆ Examen médico
◆ Evidencia de apoyo financiera por prometido/a
◆ Evidencia de relaciones válidas con el/la prometido/a
◆ Fotografías (como en el caso de naturalización)

Es necesario que los dos prometidos, estadounidense y extranjero, estén capaces y dispuestos a entrar en matrimonio válido en los Estados Unidos. Quizás te parece obvio este punto, pero hay gente que intenta abusar esta ruta hacia la ciudadanía porque es más corta. Es necesario que los dos prometidos se hayan visto físicamente dentro de los dos años anteriores—otro requisito aparentemente obvio y extraño, pero también opone actos fraudulentos. Hay casos en que el *Attorney General* puede ignorar (*waive*) la regla—si los prometidos han sido separados por una guerra, por ejemplo.

☆ **FRAUD:** un engaño practicado deliberadamente para ganar una ventaja ilegal o injusto

Tan pronto como la solicitud esté completa y el solicitante tenga todos los documentos requisitos, un oficial consular lo entrevistará. Si es por fin elegible, le dará una visa que admite una entrada dentro de un período de seis meses. Hay que pagar un honorario de $165. Para más

información sobre visas estadounidenses, estas páginas de Web son
útiles:

- ◆ www.travel.state.gov
- ◆ www.uscis.gov
- ◆ www.usavisanow.com

Después de entrar en los Estados Unidos

El prometido extranjero debe buscar permiso para trabajar al
contactar a USCIS. Este paso significa que el gobierno quiere que
cada residente nuevo se haga parte productiva de la economía
estadounidense.

Entonces, el matrimonio ha de tener lugar dentro de 90 días.
Después del matrimonio, el esposo extranjero tiene que solicitar un
cambio de estatus: debe hacerse *Legal Permanent Resident* a través de
los formularios I-485 y I-130. Si se aceptan, USCIS le dará el estatus
de "residencia permanente condicional" por dos años. Después de
estos dos años, el extranjero puede solicitar que se quite el estatus
"condicional" (a través del formulario I-751) si presenta evidencia
de que el matrimonio todavía está en efecto (que no se han divorci-
ado). En este punto, el esposo extranjero casi tiene la ciudadanía
estadounidense.

Familiares

Los hijos no casados que tienen menos de 18 años de un prometido
extranjero adquieren estatus K-2 no inmigratoria *si se nombran en el
formulario de solicitud*. Un formulario distinto se requiere si los hijos
llegan dentro de un año después de que se expida la visa K-1. Después
de un año, se requiere otra solicitud de visa.

¿Sabes que . . .

... el esposo de un ciudadano estadounidense puede solicitar la naturalización después de haber vivido tres años en

los Estados Unidos—con tal que cumpla con todos los requisitos de física, de residencia y de naturalización? Hay excepciones si el residente permanente está casado con en un ciudadano estadounidense que está fuera del país en el empleo de

> ➤ el gobierno estadounidense (incluye las Fuerzas Armadas)
> ➤ institutos estadounidenses de recerca reconocidos por el *Attorney General*
> ➤ organizaciones religiosas estadounidenses reconocidas
> ➤ firmas estadounidenses que desarrollan el comercio de los Estados Unidos—o ciertas organizaciones internacionales que envuelven los Estados Unidos

Si crees que una de estas excepciones te aplica, ponte en contacto con USCIS para más información.

Desafortunadamente, la ruta hacia la ciudadanía por medio del matrimonio has sido abusado tantas veces que el gobierno estadounidense ha tratado de complicar el proceso; como consecuencia, puede ser muy confuso. Si es posible, habla con un abogado—o una persona que se hizo ciudadano a través del mismo proceso—para evitar dificultades en obtener una visa K-1.

Ciudadanía para hijos adoptivos o extranjeros de ciudadanos estadounidenses

Si piensas en adoptar a hijos, lee con cuidado. Los niños adoptivos que nacieron fuera de los Estados Unidos pueden hacerse ciudadanos estadounidenses automáticamente (bajo el *Child Citizenship Act* (CCA) del año de 2000) o al enviar el formulario USCIS N-600 o N-600K antes de que cumplan 18 años. Mira la página de Web de USCIS para más información.

Ciudadanía automática

La mayoría de hijos adoptivos que nacieron fuera de los Estados Unidos se hacen ciudadanos el día en que llegan a los Estados Unidos. Según USCIS, hay unos requisitos que cumplir para que transcurra así:

◆ Al menos un padre adoptivo tiene que ser ciudadano estadounidense
◆ Es necesario que el hijo tenga menos de 18 años de edad
◆ La adopción ha de estar completa y finalizada
◆ Es necesario que el hijo esté presente en los Estados Unidos como residente permanente

(o que tenga un *Grant of Citizenship* automático—*Citizenship by Application* si el hijo vive fuera de este país)

Si se satisfacen todos los requisitos, el hijo es un ciudadano automático de los Estados Unidos.

Solicitar la ciudadanía por parte de un niño

Si no se satisfacen los requisitos "automáticos", es necesario que el padre solicite la ciudadanía del hijo. Si el padre es ciudadano estadounidense, usará el formulario N-600.

Si el padre es residente permanente y no ciudadano, solicitará ciudadanía para el hijo **sólo** cuando busca su propia ciudadanía. En este caso, el padre rellenará el formulario como se describió antes, pero incluirá el formulario N-600.

No te olvides que estas reglas aplican solamente a los hijos que tienen menos de 18 años. Hijos adoptivos con más de 18 años tienen que solicitar la ciudadanía sin ayuda familiar, según el proceso que se describe en los primeros capítulos.

¿Sabes que . . .

... bajo el *Child Citizenship Act* de 2000, ciertos hijos residentes que nacieron fuera de los Estados Unidos pueden lograr la ciudadanía automáticamente?

Estos hijos **no** tienen que solicitar la ciudadanía. La reciben el día en que cumplen con todos los requisitos. Pero no reciben *evidencia* automáticamente de haber logrado ciudadanía. Para obtener tal evidencia, los padres deben pedir un *Certificate of Citizenship* del USCIS. Se necesita este certificado para obtener un pasaporte.

Si ambos padres de un hijo que nació en otro país son ciudadanos estadounidenses, y si al menos un padre vivía en los Estados Unidos antes de que naciera el hijo, el hijo recibirá ciudadanía. Los padres deben solicitar un *Certificate of Citizenship* (Formulario N-600) para su hijo; es evidencia de la ciudadanía del hijo, más o menos como un certificado de nacimiento. Además, bajo el *Child Citizen Act,* una ley que se promulgó el 27 de febrero de 2001, los hijos adoptivos (con menos de 18 años) de ciudadanos estadounidenses logran ciudadanía automáticamente el día que llegan a los Estados Unidos. Si viven en otro país, tienen que solicitar ciudadanía. Esta nueva ley protege a los hijos extranjeros de ciudadanos estadounidenses de ser deportados.

Ciudadanía dual

Cuando se dice que una persona tiene ciudadanía dual, quiere decir que es ciudadano de dos países distintos a la vez. Hay personas cuyos padres tienen nacionalidades diferentes, y como consecuencia tienen automáticamente ciudadanía dual. Hay otras personas extranjeras que mantienen su ciudadanía natal después de hacerse ciudadanos estadounidenses.

Cada país tiene sus propias leyes de ciudadanía—hay varios países en que no se permite la ciudadanía dual. Lo siguiente es una lista de países que sí la permiten—con excepción de los que tienen regulaciones especiales. La lista se basa en la información más precisa al tiempo de publicación; debes averiguar si tu país natal permite la ciudadanía dual antes de solicitar naturalización.

Países que normalmente reconoce la ciudadanía dual

África del Sur	Francia	Nigeria
Albania	Ghana	Nueva Zelanda
Alemania	Grecia	Panamá
Antigua y Barbuda	Grenada	Paraguay
Argentina	Guatemala	Perú
Australia	Haití	Pitcairn
Bahamas	Holanda	Polonia
Bangla Desh	Hungría	Portugal
Barbados	India	Reino Unido
Belize	Irán	República
Benin	Irlanda	Dominicana
Bolivia	Irlanda del Norte	Rumania
Brasil	Israel	Rusia
Bulgaria	Italia	Santo Kitts y
Burkina Faso	Jamaica	Nevis
Cabo Verde	Jordania	Santa Lucía
Camboya	Letonia	San Vincente
Canadá	Líbano	Serbia (Yugoslavia)
Chile	Lesoto	Slovenia
Chipre	Liechtenstein	Sri Lanka
Chipre (Norte)	Lituania	Suecia
Colombia	Macao (w/ Portugal)	Suiza
Costa Rica	Macedonia	Tailandia
Croacia	Madagascar	Taiwan
Dominica	Malta	Trinidad y
Ecuador	Marruecos	Tobago
Egipto	México	Tíbet
El Salvador	Montenegro	Turquía
Estados Unidos	(Yugoslavia)	Ucrania
Filipinas	Mongolia	Uruguay
Fiyi	Nicaragua	Viet Nam

¿Sabes que . . .

… sin tener en cuenta el estatus ciudadano de sus padres, *todos* los hijos que nacen en los Estados Unidos son ciudadanos?

Embajadas en los Estados Unidos

Si tienes preguntas sobre la ciudadanía dual o tu visa, u otras cuestiones del proceso de naturalización y si quieres hablar con alguien que tenga conocimiento específico de tu país natal, ponte en contacto con su embajada en los Estados Unidos. El Apéndice A contiene una lista de embajadas.

Para concluir . . .

Como ya ves, hay muchas excepciones y casos especiales a través del proceso de naturalización. Es posible que tengas algunas dificultades; es posible que algunas excepciones te apliquen y otras no. De cualquier forma, es importante que sepas que existen para poder decidir qué hacer. En cualquier momento del proceso, si te está confuso, busca ayuda profesional; ponte en contacto con tu embajada, tu abogado o USCIS.

☆ ☆ ☆

LA HISTORIA DE CARLA:

HACERSE UN ciudadano del mundo: Una nota para los padres estadounidenses con hijos extranjeros

¡Felicitaciones! Después que se disminuye la emoción de dar a luz un bebé, los padres tienen que empezar a superar muchísimo "*red tape*" burocrático por lo que se refiere a establecer la identidad oficial del hijo. Es cierto que puede ser un proceso complicado. Muchos hijos nacidos en la década pasada o tienen padres con nacionalidades diferentes o nacieron fuera de los Estados Unidos. Nuestras hijas tenían complicaciones extras: nacieron en Europa a padres expatriados—una madre estadounidense y un padre canadiense. Puede ser que, en nuestro mundo tecnológico, la geografía se pone irrelevante, pero no es así con respeto a la burocracia. Es obvio que la política no lleva el mismo paso que la globalización, y el caso de la ciudadanía dual puede ser problemático.

Es casi imposible tener todos los detalles sobre la ciudadanía de hijos recién nacidos en todos los países—las reglas siempre están cambiando, y es casi cierto que cambiarán de nuevo antes de que tu hijo necesite una foto de pasaporte. No te olvides, sin embargo, que la política y el proceso concreto no son la misma cosa—y, además, que la política en muchas instancias se contradice. Por eso, he hecho un resumen de las políticas de cuatro países—los que nos estaban relevantes durante el proceso—para ilustrar la complejidad del proceso y dar unos consejos basados en la experiencia personal.

☆ RECIPROCAL: intercambiable; complementano

ESTADOS UNIDOS

La política existente de la embajada americana en Canadá dice: "Cuando una persona se naturaliza en otro país (o de otro modo tiene otra nacionalidad), y después se revela que no ha perdido la ciudadanía estadounidense, es posible que la persona mantenga ciudadanía dual. Es prudente, sin embargo, preguntar a oficiales del otro país para averiguar si se permite la ciudadanía dual. Los Estados Unidos no prefiere la ciudadanía dual, pero sí la reconoce en ciertos casos." Es decir que el gobierno estadounidense más o menos ignora tales casos. No es necesario que el gobierno sepa tu estatus a menos que quiera renunciar tu ciudadanía estadounidense. ¿Por qué querría alguien renunciarla? Para alguna gente, es inconveniente tener que pagar impuestos a través de la vida en dos países. En los Estados Unidos, la responsabilidad de pagar impuestos se basa en la ciudadanía, no en la presencia física en el país.

El proceso en los Estados Unidos de obtener la ciudadanía para un recién nacido es más o menos lógico. Envuelve tres solicitudes distintas: Certificado de Nacimiento Extranjero, pasaporte y número de Seguridad Social. El primero y el segundo se satisfacen cuando nace el bebé, pero el tercero puede requerir que esperes seis meses. Tendrás que presentar a tu hijo en el consulado y jurar que toda la información en tu solicitud está correcta. Para mí fue chistoso que el formulario requiere que escribas detalles como color de pelo. Todos los bebés son calvos, ¿no? De cualquier forma, ¡el pasaporte está válido por cinco años!

El único aspecto difícil puede ser evidenciar que has vivido en los Estados Unidos por cinco años consecutivos después de cumplir 14 años. La regla existe porque ha habido una serie de secuestros. Los consulados y embajadas respetan estas reglas; son muy serias, y tienes que estar dispuesto a respetarlas igualmente.

CANADÁ

Hay semejanzas entre la política canadiense y la estadounidense, y el proceso también es más o menos lógico, pero se requiere un período más largo para completar. El pasaporte canadiense está válido unos diez años, así que tu hijo tendrá una foto embarazosa por una década.

ALEMANIA

Mi hija mayor nació en Alemania, pero podía desde el principio solicitar ciudadanía estadounidense y canadiense a causa de sus padres sin haber ido a ninguno de los dos países. Pero, *no* podía solicitar ciudadanía alemana—porque la nacionalidad alemana, hasta el día actual, se define por la sangre. Si una persona es de ascendencia alemana, tiene derecho legal de ciudadanía alemana. No sé mucho más, porque no le aplicaba a mi hija. Tal vez quisiera notar, sin embargo, que en Alemania la participación militar es un requisito; si a ti no te gusta esta regla, puede ser que debas buscar la ciudadanía solamente en países donde el servicio militar es voluntario.

ESPAÑA

En España, si los dos padres son de países fuera de Europa, entonces un hijo no puede obtener un pasaporte español cuando nace. Pero si el hijo tiene residencia legal en España por dos años, sus padres tienen la opción de solicitar un pasaporte. Es proscrito en España poseer pasaportes de más de una nación; el hijo tendrá que renunciar los otros que tenga. Vivo en España, pero no sé que mi familia y yo nos quedamos aquí y no quiero solicitar un pasaporte para mi hija hasta que decidamos. Pero sabemos que puede ser útil tener un pasaporte de la Unión Europea desde una perspectiva puramente profesional.

¿Estás desconcertado? No te preocupes—no eres el único. Aquí tienes unos consejos básicos para sobrevivir el proceso, no obstante en qué países solicitas ciudadanía para tus hijos:

◆ Manten organizados y accesibles todos los registros oficiales.

◆ Siempre conserva las versiones originales de pasaportes, certificados y otras cosas legales.

◆ Está dispuesto a sacar muchas fotos de tu hijo recién nacido: cuando tengas una foto buena, tendrás que convertirla en la forma correcta (¡que *no* es la misma de país a país!).

◆ Está dispuesto a pagar honorarios en varios momentos del proceso—quizás para traducir documentos.

◆ Asegura que tienes toda la información actual sobre las reglas, que continúan cambiando.

◆ Ten paciencia.

Para concluir, espero que no tengas miedo de ningún aspecto. Tu bebé tendrá una identidad una vez que se complete todo el papeleo. Todo esto vale la pena: la experiencia de tener ciudadanía dual es un privilegio útil. Y es claro que das a tu hijo varias ventajas, desde un punto de vista personal y profesional. Como el mundo se hace más interdependiente cada día, la nacionalidad dual continuará siendo más útil que no. Como mínimo, le introducirá a tu hijo una conciencia internacional—una cualidad excelente en no obstante su trayectoria en la vida. Esperamos sobre todo que la gente de ciudadanía dual promoverá una comprensión mutua entre naciones.

Contactos útiles

Oficinas USCIS municipales y regionales

USCIS tiene una página de Web bien comprehensiva: incluye direcciones, números de teléfono y otra información fundamental sobre oficinas por toda la nación. Para lograr acceso a la página, busca www.uscis.gov.

También puedes llamar a USCIS gratis a **1-800-375-5283** o **1-800-767-1833 (TTY)**.

Esto es una lista, organizada por estado, de oficinas municipales y regionales:

ALABAMA
Atlanta, Georgia District Office
Martin Luther King Jr. Federal Building
77 Forsyth Street, SW
Atlanta, GA 30303

ALASKA
Anchorage
620 East 10th Avenue
Suite 10
Anchorage, AL 99501

ARIZONA
Phoenix
2035 North Central Avenue
Phoenix, AZ 85004

Tucson
6431 South Country Club Road
Tucson, AZ 85706-5907
(Suboffice serving Cochise, Pima, Santa
  Cruz, Graham, and Pinal.)

ARKANSAS
Fort Smith
4977 Old Greenwood Road
Fort Smith, AR 72903
(Suboffice serving western Arkansas. The
  district office is located in New Orleans.)

CALIFORNIA
Los Angeles
300 North Los Angeles Street
Room 1001
Los Angeles, CA 90012
(District office serving Los Angeles,
  Orange, Riverside, San Bernardino,
  Santa Barbara, San Luis Obispo, and
  Ventura counties. There are also offices
  in East Los Angeles, El Monte, Bell,
  Bellflower, Westminster, Santa Ana,
  Camarillo, Riverside, San Pedro, Los
  Angeles International Airport, Lompoc,
  and Lancaster.)

San Bernardino
655 West Rialto Avenue
San Bernardino, CA 92410-3327

San Diego
880 Front Street
Suite 1234
San Diego, CA 92101
(District office serving San Diego and
  Imperial counties.)

San Francisco
444 Washington Street
San Francisco, CA 94111
(District office serving Alameda, Contra
  Costa, Del Norte, Humboldt, Lake,
  Marin, Mendocino, Napa, San Francisco,
  San Mateo, Sonoma, and Trinity.)

Fresno
1177 Fulton Mall
Fresno, CA 93721-1913
(Suboffice serving Fresno, Inyo, Kern,
  Kings, Madera, Mariposa, Merced,
  Mono, and Tulare.)

Sacramento
650 Capitol Mall
Sacramento, CA 95814
(Suboffice serving Alpine, Amador,
  Butte, Calaveras, Colusa, El Dorado,
  Glenn, Lassen, Modoc, Nevada, Placer,
  Plumas, Sacramento, San Joaquin,
  Shasta, Sierra, Sutter, Siskiyou,
  Solano, Tehama, Tuolumne, Yolo, and
  Yuba.)

San Jose
1887 Monterey Road
San Jose, CA 95112
(Suboffice serving Monterey, San Benito,
  Santa Clara, and Santa Cruz.)

Santa Ana
34 Civic Center Plaza
Federal Building
Santa Ana, CA 92701

COLORADO
Denver
4730 Paris Street
Denver, CO 80239

CONNECTICUT
Hartford
450 Main Street
4th Floor
Hartford, CT 06103-3060
(Suboffice serving Connecticut. The district office is located in Boston.)

DELAWARE
Dover
1305 McD Drive
Dover, DE 19901
(Satellite office. District office is in Philadelphia.)

DISTRICT OF COLUMBIA (WASHINGTON, D.C.)
2675 Propensity Avenue
Fairfax, VA 22031
(District office serving the entire state of Virginia and the District of Columbia)

FLORIDA
Miami
7880 Biscayne Boulevard
Miami, FL 33138
(District office)

Jacksonville
4121 Southpoint Boulevard
Jacksonville, FL 32216
(Suboffice serving Alachua, Baker, Bay, Bradford, Calhoun, Clay, Columbia, Dixie, Duval, Escambia, Franklin, Gadsden, Gilchrist, Gulf, Hamilton, Holmes, Jackson, Jefferson, Lafayette, Leon, Levy, Liberty, Madison, Nassau, Okaloosa, Putnum, Santa Rosa, St. Johns, Suwanee, Taylor, Union, Wakulla, Walton, and Washington.)

Orlando
9403 Tradeport Drive
Orlando, FL 32827
(Suboffice serving Orange, Osceola, Seminole, Lake, Brevard, Flagler, Volusia, Marion, and Sumter.)

Tampa
5524 West Cypress Street
Tampa, FL 33607-1708
(Suboffice serving Citrus, Hernando, Pasco, Pinellas, Hillsborough, Polk, Hardee, Manatee, Sarasota, De Soto, Charlotte, and Lee.)

West Palm Beach
326 Fern Street,
Suite 200
West Palm Beach, FL 33401
(Suboffice serving Palm Beach, Martin, St. Lucie, Indian River, Okeechobee, Hendry, Glades, and Highland counties.)

GEORGIA
Atlanta
Martin Luther King Jr. Federal Building
77 Forsyth Street, SW
Atlanta, GA 30303

GUAM
Agana
Sirena Plaza
108 Hernan Cortez Avenue
Suite 100
Hagatna, Guam 96910
(Suboffice serving Guam and the Northern Mariana Islands. District office is located in Honolulu.)

HAWAII
Honolulu
595 Ala Moana Boulevard
Honolulu, HI 96813
(District office serving Hawaii, the
  Territory of Guam, and the
  Commonwealth of Northern Marianas.)

IDAHO
Boise
1185 South Vinnell Way
Room 108
Boise, ID 83709
(Suboffice serving southwest and south
  central Idaho. The district office is
  located in Helena, Montana.)

ILLINOIS
Chicago
101 West Congress Parkway
Chicago, IL 60605

INDIANA
Indianapolis
950 North Meridian Street
Room 400
Indianapolis, IN 46204-3915
(Suboffice serving the state of Indiana
  except Lake, Porter, LaPorte, and
  St. Joseph counties in northwest
  Indiana. Residents of those four
  counties are served by the Chicago
  district office.)

IOWA
Des Moines
210 Walnut Street
Room 369
Federal Building
Des Moines, IA 50309
(Satellite office. The district office is
  located in Omaha, Nebraska.)

KANSAS
Wichita
271 West 3rd Street North
Suite 1050
Wichita, KS 67202-1212
(Satellite office serving western Kansas.
  The district office is located in Kansas
  City, Missouri.)

KENTUCKY
Louisville
USCIS-Louisville
Room 390
601 West Broadway
Louisville, KY 40202
(Suboffice serving Kentucky.)

LOUISIANA
New Orleans
Metairie Centre
2424 Edenbom Avenue
Third Floor (Suite 300)
Metairie, LA 70001
(Serving Louisiana, Arkansas,
  Tennessee, and Kentucky.)

MAINE
Portland
176 Gannett Drive
South Portland, ME 04106
(Serving Maine and Vermont.)

MARYLAND
Baltimore
Fallon Federal Building
31 Hopkins Plaza
Baltimore, MD 21201

MASSACHUSETTS
Boston
John F. Kennedy Federal Building
Government Center
Boston, MA 02203

MICHIGAN
Detroit
333 Mt. Elliott
Detroit, MI 48207

MINNESOTA
St. Paul
2901 Metro Drive
Suite 100
Bloomington, MN 55425
(Serving Minnesota, North Dakota, and
South Dakota.)

MISSISSIPPI
New Orleans District Office (see
Louisiana)

MISSOURI
Kansas City
9747 Northwest Conant Avenue
Kansas City, MO 64153
(District office serving Missouri and
Kansas.)

St. Louis
Robert A. Young Federal Building
1222 Spruce Street
Room 1.100
St. Louis, Missouri 63103-2815
(Suboffice serving eastern part of
Missouri.)

MONTANA
Helena
2800 Skyway Drive
Helena, MT 59602
(District office for Montana and portions
of Idaho.)

NEBRASKA
Omaha
1717 Avenue H
Omaha, NE 68110-2752
(District office serving Nebraska and Iowa.)

NEVADA
Las Vegas
3373 Pepper Lane
Las Vegas, NV 89120-2739
(Suboffice serving Clark, Esmeralda,
Nye, and Lincoln counties. The district
office is located in Phoenix, AZ.)

Reno
1351 Corporate Boulevard
Reno, NV 89502
(Suboffice servicing Carson, Churchill,
Douglas, Elko, Eureka, Humboldt,
Lander, Lyon, Mineral, Pershing, Storey,
Washoe, and White Pine counties.)

NEW HAMPSHIRE
Manchester
803 Canal Street
Manchester, NH 03101

NEW JERSEY
Newark
970 Broad Street
Newark, NJ 07102
(District office serving Bergen, Essex,
Hudson, Hunterdon, Middlesex, Morris,
Passaic, Somerset, Sussex, Union, and
Warren counties.)

Cherry Hill
1886 Greentree Road
Cherry Hill, NJ 08003
(Suboffice serving Atlantic, Burlington,
Camden, Cape May, Cumberland,
Gloucester, Mercer, Monmouth,
Ocean, and Salem counties.)

NEW MEXICO
Albuquerque
1720 Randolph Road, SE
Albuquerque, NM 87106
(Suboffice serving northern New Mexico.
The district office is located in El Paso,
Texas.)

NEW YORK
Buffalo
Federal Center
130 Delaware Avenue
Buffalo, NY 14202
(District office serving the state of
New York, with the exception of
New York City and its surrounding
counties.)

New York City
26 Federal Plaza
New York, NY 10278
(District office serving the five
boroughs of New York City,
Nassau, Suffolk, Dutchess,
Orange, Putnam, Rockland,
Sullivan, Ulster, and Westchester
counties.)

Albany
1086 Troy-Schenectady Road
Latham, New York 12110
(Suboffice serving Albany, Broome,
Chenango, Clinton, Columbia,
Delaware, Essex, Franklin, Fulton,
Greene, Hamilton, Herkimer,
Madison, Montgomery, Oneida,
Otsego, Rensselaer,
Saint Lawrence, Saratoga,
Schenectady, Schoharie,
Tioga, Warren, and
Washington.)

NORTH CAROLINA
Charlotte
6130 Tyvola Centre Drive
Charlotte, NC 28217
(Suboffice serving North Carolina.
The district office is located in
Atlanta.)

NORTH DAKOTA
St. Paul, Minnesota District Office
2901 Metro Drive
Suite 100
Bloomington, MN 55425

OHIO
Cleveland
AJC Federal Building
1240 East Ninth Street
Room 501
Cleveland, OH 44199
(District office serving the northern part
of Ohio.)

Cincinnati
J.W. Peck Federal Building
550 Main Street
Room 4001
Cincinnati, OH 45202
(Suboffice serving the southern part of
Ohio.)

Columbus
Leveque Tower
50 West Broad Street
Suite 306
Columbus, OH 43215

OKLAHOMA
Oklahoma City
4400 SW 44th Street
Suite "A"
Oklahoma City, OK 73119-2800
(Suboffice serving Oklahoma. District
office is located in Dallas.)

OREGON
Portland
511 NW Broadway
Portland, OR 97209
(District office serving Oregon.)

PENNSYLVANIA
Philadelphia
1600 Callowhill Street
Philadelphia, PA 19130
(District office for Pennsylvania,
Delaware, and West Virginia.)

Pittsburgh
300 Sidney Street
Pittsburgh, PA 15203
(Suboffice serving western Pennsylvania
and West Virginia.)

PUERTO RICO
San Juan
San Patricio Office Center
7 Tabonuco Street
Suite 100
Guaynabo, PR 00968
(District office serving Puerto Rico and
the U.S. Virgin Islands.)

RHODE ISLAND
Providence
200 Dyer Street
Providence, RI 02903
(Suboffice serving Rhode Island. The
district office is located in Boston.)

SOUTH CAROLINA
Charleston
1 Poston Road
Suite 130
Parkshore Center
Charleston, SC 29407
(Suboffice serving South Carolina. The
district office is located in Atlanta.)

SOUTH DAKOTA
St. Paul, Minnesota District Office
2901 Metro Drive
Suite 100
Bloomington, MN 55425

TENNESSEE*
Memphis
842 Virginia Pen Cove
Memphis, TN 38122
(Suboffice serving the eastern half of
Arkansas, the northern half of
Mississippi, and the state of
Tennessee. The district office is
located in New Orleans.)
*(Naturalization cases in Anderson,
Bedford, Bledsoe, Blount, Bradley,
Campbell, Carter, Claiborne, Cocke,
Coffee, Franklin, Grainger, Greene,
Grundy, Hamblen, Hamilton, Hancock,
Hawkins, Jefferson, Johnson, Knox,
Lincoln, Loudon, Marion, McMinn,
Meigs, Monroe, Moore, Morgan, Polk,
Rhea, Roane, Scott, Sequatchie, Sevier,
Sullivan, Unicoi, Union, Van Buren,
Warren, and Washington counties fall
under the jurisdiction of the Louisville,
Kentucky suboffice.)

TEXAS
Dallas
8101 North Stemmons Freeway
Dallas, TX 75247
(District office serving 123 northern
counties in the state of Texas and all
of Oklahoma.)

El Paso
1545 Hawkins Boulevard
Suite 167
El Paso, TX 79925
(District office serving West Texas and
New Mexico.)

Harlingen
1717 Zoy Street
Harlingen, TX 78552
(District office serving Brooks, Cameron,
Hidalgo, Kennedy, Kleberg, Starr, and
Willacy.)

Houston
126 Northpoint
Houston, TX 77060
(District office serving southeastern
   Texas.)

San Antonio
8940 Fourwinds Drive
San Antonio, TX 78239
(District office serving central and south
   Texas.)

UTAH
Salt Lake City
5272 South College Drive, #100
Murray, UT 84123
(Suboffice serving Utah. The district
   office is located in Denver.)

VERMONT
St. Albans
64 Gricebrook Road
St. Albans, VT 05478
(Suboffice serving Vermont and New
   Hampshire. The district office is locat-
   ed in Portland, Maine.)

U.S. VIRGIN ISLANDS
Charlotte Amalie
8000 Nisky Center
Suite 1A First Floor South
Charlotte Amalie,
St. Thomas, USVI 00802
(Suboffice serving St. Thomas and St.
   John. The district office is located in
   San Juan.)

St. Croix
Sunny Isle Shopping Center
Christiansted
St. Croix, USVI 00823
(Suboffice serving St. Croix, U.S. Virgin
   Islands. The district office is located in
   San Juan.)

VIRGINIA
Norfolk
5280 Henneman Drive
Norfolk, Virginia 23513
(Suboffice serving southeastern Virginia.
   The district office is located in
   Washington, D.C.)

WASHINGTON
Seattle
12500 Tukwila International Boulevard
Seattle WA 98168
(District office serving Washington, and
   ten northern counties in Idaho.)

Spokane
U.S. Courthouse
920 West Riverside
Room 691
Spokane, WA 99201
(Suboffice serving Adams, Benton,
   Chelan, Asotin, Columbia, Douglas,
   Ferry, Garfield, Grant, Lincoln,
   Okanogan, Pend O'reille, Spokane,
   Stevens, Walla Walla, and
   Whitman.)

Yakima
415 North Third Street
Yakima, WA 98901
(Suboffice serving Kittitas, Klickitat, and
   Yakima.)

WISCONSIN
Milwaukee
310 East Knapp Street
Milwaukee, WI 53202
(Suboffice serving Wisconsin. The
   district office is located in
   Chicago.)

International Embassies in the United States

The Republic of Afghanistan
2341 Wyoming Avenue NW
Washington, D.C. 20008
Tel: 202-483-6410
Fax: 202-483-6488
www.embassyofafghanistan.org

The Republic of Albania
2100 S Street NW
Washington, D.C. 20008
Tel: 202-223-4942
Fax: 202-628-7342
www.albaniaembassy.org

The Democratic and Popular Republic of Algeria
2118 Kalorama Road NW
Washington, D.C. 20008
Tel: 202-265-2800
Fax: 202-667-2174
www.algeria-us.org

The Embassy of The Republic of Angola
1615 M Street NW
Suite 900
Washington, D.C. 20036
Tel: 202-785-1156
Fax: 202-785-1258

Embassy of Antigua and Barbuda
3216 New Mexico Avenue NW
Washington, D.C. 20016
Tel: 202-362-5122
Fax: 202-362-5225

The Argentine Republic
1600 New Hampshire Avenue NW
Washington, D.C. 20009
Tel: 202-238-6400
Fax: 202-332-3171
www.embassyofargentina.us

Embassy of the Republic of Armenia
2225 R Street
Washington, D.C. 20008
Tel: 202-319-1976
Fax: 202-319-2982
www.armeniaemb.org

Embassy of Australia
1601 Massachusetts Avenue NW
Washington, D.C. 20036
Tel: 202-797-3000
Fax: 202-797-3168
www.austemb.org

Austrian Press & Information Service
3524 International Court NW
Washington, D.C. 20008-3035
Tel: 202-895-6700
Fax: 202-895-6750
www.austria.org

The Republic of Azerbaijan
927 15th Street NW
Suite 700
Washington, D.C. 20035
Tel: 202-337-3500
Fax: 202-337-5911
www.azembassy.us

The Commonwealth of the Bahamas
2220 Massachusetts Avenue NW
Washington, D.C. 20008
Tel: 202-319-2660
Fax: 202-319-2668

Embassy of the State of Bahrain
3502 International Drive NW
Washington, D.C. 20008
Tel: 202-342-0741
Fax: 202-362-2192
www.bahrainembassy.org

The People's Republic of Bangladesh
3510 International Drive NW
Washington, D.C. 20008
Tel: 202-244-2745
Fax: 202-244-5366
www.bangladoot.org/

Barbados
2144 Wyoming Avenue NW
Washington, D.C. 20008
Tel: 202-939-9200
Fax: 202-332-7467

Embassy of the Republic of Belarus
1619 New Hampshire Avenue NW
Washington, D.C. 20009
Tel: 202-986-1606
Fax: 202-986-1805
www.belarusembassy.org

Embassy of Belgium
3330 Garfield Street NW
Washington, D.C. 20008
Tel: 202-333-6900
Fax: 202-333-3079
www.diplobel.us

Belize
2535 Massachusetts Avenue NW
Washington, D.C. 20008
Tel: 202-332-9636
Fax: 202-332-6888
www.embassyofbelize.org

Embassy of the Republic of Benin
2124 Kalorama Road NW
Washington, D.C. 20008
Tel: 202-232-6656
Fax: 202-265-1996

Bolivia
3014 Massachusetts Avenue NW
Washington, D.C. 20008
Tel: 202-483-4410
Fax: 202-328-3712
www.bolivia-usa.org

Embassy of Bosnia and Herzegovina
2109 E Street NW
Washington, D.C. 20037
Tel: 202-337-1500
Fax: 202-337-1502
www.bosnianembassy.org

Botswana
1531-3 New Hampshire Avenue NW
Washington, D.C. 20036
Tel: 202-244-4990
Fax: 202-244-4164
www.botswanaembassy.org

Brazil
3006 Massachusetts Avenue NW
Washington, D.C. 20008
Tel: 202-238-2700
Fax: 202-238-2827
www.brasilemb.org/

Embassy of Brunei Darussalam
3520 International Court NW
Washington, D.C. 20008
Tel: 202-237-1838
Fax: 202-885-0560
www.bruneiembassy.org

Embassy of Burkina Faso
2340 Massachusetts Avenue NW
Washington, D.C. 20008
Tel: 202-332-5577
Fax: 202-667-1882
www.burkinaembassy-usa.org

The Republic of Bulgaria
1621 22nd Street NW
Washington, D.C. 20008
Tel: 202-387-0174
Fax: 202-234-7973
www.bulgaria-embassy.org

Embassy of the Republic of Burundi
2233 Wisconsin Avenue NW
Suite 212
Washington, D.C. 20007
Tel: 202-342-2574
Fax: 202-342-2578
www.burundiembassy-usa.org

Embassy of the Republic of Cameroon
2349 Massachusetts Avenue NW
Washington, D.C. 20008
Tel: 202-265-8790
Fax: 202-387-3826

Royal Embassy of Camodia
4500 16th Street NW
Washington, D.C. 20011
Tel: 202-726-7742
Fax: 202-726-8381
www.embassyofcambodia.org

Canada
501 Pennsylvania Avenue NW
Washington, D.C. 20001
Tel: 202-682-1740
Fax: 202-682-7726
www.canadianembassy.org

The Republic of Cape Verde
3415 Massachusetts Avenue NW
Washington, D.C. 20007
Tel: 202-965-6820
Fax: 202-965-1207
www.capeverdeusa.org

The Central African Republic
1618 22nd Street NW
Washington, D.C. 20008
Tel: 202-483-7800
Fax: 202-332-9893

The Republic of Chad
2002 R Street NW
Washington, D.C. 20009
Tel: 202-462-4009
Fax: 202-265-1937
www.chadembassy.org

Chile
1732 Massachusetts Avenue NW
Washington, D.C. 20036
Tel: 202-785-1746
Fax: 202-887-5579
www.chile-usa.org

Embassy of the People's Republic of China
2300 Connecticut Avenue NW
Washington, D.C. 20008
Tel: 202-328-2500
Fax: 202-588-0032
www.china-embassy.org

The Embassy of Columbia
2118 Leroy Place NW
Washington, D.C. 20008
Tel: 202-387-8338
Fax: 202-232-8643
www.colombiaemb.net

The Republic of Congo
4891 Colorado Avenue NW
Washington, D.C. 20011
Tel: 202-726-5500
Fax: 202-726-1860
www.embassyofcongo.org

Embassy of the Democratic Republic of Congo
1800 New Hampshire Avenue NW
Washington, D.C. 20009
Tel: 202-234-7690
Fax: 202-234-2609

Embassy of Costa Rica
2114 S Street NW
Washington, D.C. 20008
Tel: 202-234-2945
Fax: 202-265-4795
www.costarica-embassy.org

The Republic of Cote d'Ivoire (Ivory Coast)
2424 Massachusetts Avenue NW
Washington, D.C. 20008
Tel: 202-797-0300

The Embassy of the Republic of Croatia
2343 Massachusetts Avenue NW
Washington, D.C. 20008
Tel: 202-588-5899
Fax: 202-588-8936
www.croatiaemb.org

Cuba Interests Section
2630 and 2639 16th Street NW
Washington, D.C. 20009
Tel: 202-797-8518
Fax: 202-986-7283

The Republic of Cyprus
2211 R Street NW
Washington, D.C. 20008
Tel: 202-462-5772
Fax: 202-483-6710
www.cyprusembassy.net

Embassy of the Czech Republic
3900 Spring of Freedom Street NW
Washington, D.C. 20008
Tel: 202-274-9100
Fax: 202-966-8540
www.mzv.cz/washington

Royal Danish Embassy
3200 Whitehaven Street NW
Washington, D.C. 20008
Tel: 202-234-4300
Fax: 202-328-1470
www.denmarkemb.org

Embassy of the Republic of Djibouti
1156 15th Street NW
Suite 515
Washington, D.C. 20005
Tel: 202-331-0270
Fax: 202-331-0302

The Commonwealth of Dominica
3216 New Mexico Avenue NW
Washington, D.C. 20016
Tel: 202-364-6781
Fax: 202-364-6791

Dominican Republic
1715 22nd Street NW
Washington, D.C. 20008
Tel: 202-332-6280
Fax: 202-265-8057
www.domrep.org

Embassy of East Timor
4201 Connecticut Avenue NW
Suite 504
Washington, D.C. 20008
Tel: 202-966-3202
Fax: 202-966-3205

The Embassy of Ecuador
2535 15th Street NW
Washington, D.C. 20009
Tel: 202-234-7200
Fax: 202-667-3482

The Arab Republic of Egypt
3521 International Court NW
Washington, D.C. 20008
Tel: 202-895-5400
Fax: 202-244-4319
www.egyptembassy.us

El Salvador
2308 California Street NW
Washington, D.C. 20008
Tel: 202-265-9671
www.elsalvador.org

Equatorial Guinea
2020 16th Street NW
Washington, D.C. 20009
Tel: 202-518-5700
Fax: 202-518-5252

Embassy of Eritrea
1708 New Hampshire Avenue NW
Washington, D.C. 20009
Tel: 202-319-1991
Fax: 202-319-1304

Embassy of Estonia
1730 M Street NW
Suite 503
Washington, D.C. 20036
Tel: 202-588-0101
Fax: 202-588-0108
www.estemb.org

Embassy of Ethiopia
3506 International Drive NW
Washington, D.C. 20008
Tel: 202-364-1200
Fax: 202-686-9551
www.ethiopianembassy.org

Embassy of Fiji
2233 Wisconsin Avenue NW
Suite 240
Washington, D.C. 20007
Tel: 202-337-8320
Fax: 202-337-1996

Embassy of Finland
3301 Massachusetts Avenue NW
Washington, D.C. 20008
Tel: 202-298-5800
Fax: 202-298-6030
www.finland.org

Embassy of France
4101 Reservoir Road NW
Washington, D.C. 20007
Tel: 202-944-6000
Fax: 202-944-6072
www.info-france-usa.org

Embassy of the Gabonese Republic
2034 20th Street NW
Suite 200
Washington, D.C. 20009
Tel: 202-797-1000
Fax: 202-332-0668

Embassy of the Gambia
1155 15th Street NW
Suite 1000
Washington, D.C. 20005
Tel: 202-785-1399
Fax: 202-785-1430
www.gambia.com/index.html

The Embassy of the Republic of Georgia
1615 New Hampshire Avenue NW
Suite 300
Washington, D.C. 20009
Tel: 202-387-2390
Fax: 202-393-4537
www.georgiaemb.org

German Embassy
4645 Reservoir Road
Washington, D.C. 20007-1998
Tel: 202-298-4000
Fax: 202-298-4249 or 202-333-2653
www.germany-info.org

Ghana
3512 International Drive NW
Washington, D.C. 20008
Tel: 202 686-4520
Fax: 202-686-4527
www.ghana-embassy.org

Embassy of Greece
2221 Massachusetts Avenue NW
Washington D.C. 20008
Tel: 202-939-1300
Fax: 202-939-1324
www.greekembassy.org

Grenada
1701 New Hampshire Avenue NW
Washington, D.C. 20009
Tel: 202-265-2561
Fax: 202-265-2468
www.grenadaembassyusa.org

Guatemala
2220 R Street NW
Washington, D.C. 20008
Tel: 202-745-4952
Fax: 202-745-1908
www.guatemala-embassy.org

The Republic of Guinea
2112 Leroy Place NW
Washington, D.C. 20008
Tel: 202-986-4300

Guyana
2490 Tracy Place NW
Washington, D.C. 20008
Tel: 202-265-6900
Fax: 202-232-1297

The Republic of Haiti
2311 Massachusetts Avenue NW
Washington, D.C. 20008
Tel: 202-332-4090
Fax: 202-745-7215
www.haiti.org

The Holy See (Apostolic Nunciature)
3339 Massachusetts Avenue NW
Washington, D.C. 20008
Tel: 202-333-7121

Honduras
3007 Tilden Street NW
Suite 4M
Washington, D.C. 20008
Tel: 202-966-7702
Fax: 202-966-9751
www.hondurasemb.org

The Embassy of the Republic of Hungary
3910 Shoemaker Street NW
Washington, D.C. 20008
Tel: 202-362-6730
Fax: 202-966-8135
www.huembwas.org

Embassy of Iceland
1156 15th Street NW
Suite 1200
Washington, D.C. 20005-1704
Tel: 202-265-6653
Fax: 202-265-6656
www.iceland.org

Embassy of India

2107 Massachusetts Avenue NW
Washington, D.C. 20008
Tel: 202-939-7000
Fax: 202-265-4351
www.indianembassy.org

The Republic of Indonesia

2020 Massachusetts Avenue NW
Washington, D.C. 20036
Tel: 202-775-5200
Fax: 202-775-5365
wwwembassyofindonesia.org

Iranian Interests Section

2209 Wisconsin Avenue NW
Washington, D.C. 20007
Tel: 202-965-4990
Fax: 202-965-1073
www.daftar.org/Eng/default.asp?lang=eng

Embassy of Iraq

1801 P Street NW
Washington, D.C. 20036
Tel: 202-483-7500
Fax: 202-462-5066
www.iraqembassy.org

Ireland

2234 Massachusetts Avenue NW
Washington, D.C. 20008
Tel: 202-462-3939
Fax: 202-232-5993
www.irelandemb.org

Embassy of Israel

3514 International Drive NW
Washington, D.C. 20008
Tel: 202-364-5500
Fax: 202-364-5428
www.israelemb.org

Embassy of Italy

3000 Whitehaven Street NW
Washington, D.C. 20008
Tel: 202-612-4400
Fax: 202-518-2154
www.italyemb.org

Jamaica

1520 New Hampshire Avenue NW
Washington, D.C. 20036
Tel: 202-452-0660
Fax: 202-452-0081
www.emjamusa.org

The Embassy of Japan

2520 Massachusetts Avenue NW
Washington, D.C. 20008
Tel: 202-238-6700
Fax: 202-328-2187
www.embjapan.org

Embassy of the Hashemite Kingdom of Jordan

3504 International Drive NW
Washington, D.C. 20008
Tel: 202-966-2664
Fax: 202-966-3110
www.jordanembassyus.org

The Republic of Kazakhstan

1401 16th Street NW
Washington, D.C. 20036
Tel: 202-232-5488
Fax: 202-232-5845
www.kazakhembus.org

Embassy of Kenya

2249 R Street NW
Washington, D.C. 20008
Tel: 202-387-6101
Fax: 202-462-3829
www.kenyaembassy.com

The Republic of Korea
2450 Massachusetts Avenue NW
Washington, D.C. 20008
Tel: 202-939-5600
Fax: 202-797-0595
www.koreaembassyusa.org

The State of Kuwait
2940 Tilden Street NW
Washington, D.C. 20008
Tel: 202-966-0702
Fax: 202-364-2868

The Kyrgyz Republic
2360 Massachusetts Avenue NW
Washington, D.C. 20007
Tel: 202-338-5141
Fax: 202-395-7550
www.kgembassy.org

**The Lao People's Democratic
  Republic**
2222 S Street NW
Washington, D.C. 20008
Tel: 202-332-6416
Fax: 202-332-4923
www.laoembassy.com

Latvia
4325 17th Street NW
Washington, D.C. 20011
Tel: 202-726-8213
Fax: 202-726-6785
www.latvia-usa.org

Lebanon
2560 28th Street NW
Washington, D.C. 20008
Tel: 202-939-6300
Fax: 202-939-6324
www.lebanonembassyus.org

Embassy of Lesotho
2511 Massachusetts Avenue NW
Washington, D.C. 20008
Tel: 202-797-5533
Fax: 202-234-6815

The Republic of Liberia
5201 16th Street NW
Washington, D.C. 20011
Tel: 202-723-0437
Fax: 202-723-0436
www.embassyofliberia.org

Embassy of Liechtenstein
888 17th Street NW
Suite 1250
Washington, D.C. 20006
Tel: 202-331-0590
Fax: 202-331-3221
http://www.liechtenstein.li/en/
    fl-aussenstelle-washington-home

The Embassy of Lithuania
2622 16th Street NW
Washington, D.C. 20009-4202
Tel: 202-234-5860
Fax: 202-328-0466
www.ltembassyus.org

Luxembourg
2200 Massachusetts Avenue NW
Washington, D.C. 20008
Tel: 202-265-4171
Fax: 202-328-8270

**Embassy of the Republic of
  Macedonia**
1101 30th Street NW
Suite 302
Washington, D.C. 20007
Tel: 202-337-3063
Fax: 202-337-3093
www.macedonianembassy.org

Embassy of Madagascar
2374 Massachusetts Avenue NW
Washington, D.C. 20008
Tel: 202-265-5525
www.embassy.org/madagascar

Embassy of Malawi
2408 Massachusetts Avenue NW
Washington, D.C. 20008
Tel: 202-797-1007

Malaysia
3516 International Court NW
Washington, D.C. 20008
Tel: 202-572-9700
Fax: 202-483-7661

The Republic of Mali
2130 R Street NW
Washington, D.C. 20008
Tel: 202-332-2249
Fax: 202-332-6603
www.maliembassy-usa.org

Malta
2017 Connecticut Avenue NW
Washington, D.C. 20008
Tel: 202-462-3611
Fax: 202-387-5470
http://malta.usembassy.gov

Embassy of the Republic of the Marshall Islands
2433 Massachusetts Avenue NW
Washington, D.C. 20008
Tel: 202-234-5414
Fax: 202-232-3236
www.rmiembassyus.org

The Islamic Republic of Mauritania
2129 Leroy Place NW
Washington, D.C. 20008
Tel: 202-232-5700
Fax: 202-319-2623
http://mauritania-usa.org

Mexico
1911 Pennsylvania Avenue NW
Washington, D.C. 20006
Tel: 202-728-1600
Fax: 202-728-1698
www.embassyofmexico.org

The Federated States of Micronesia
1725 N Street NW
Washington, D.C. 20036
Tel: 202-223-4383
Fax: 202-223-4391

The Republic of Moldova
2101 S Street NW
Washington, D.C. 20008
Tel: 202-667-1130/31/37
Fax: 202-667-1204
www.embassyrm.org

Mongolia
2833 M Street NW
Washington, D.C. 20007
Tel: 202-333-7117
Fax: 202-298-9227
www.mongolianembassy.com

The Kingdom of Morocco
1601 21st Street NW
Washington, D.C. 20009
Tel: 202-462-7979
Fax: 202-265-0161

The Republic of Mozambique
1990 M Street NW
Suite 570
Washington, D.C. 20036
Tel: 202-293-7146
Fax: 202-835-0245
www.embamoc-usa.org

Embassy of the Union of Myanmar
2300 S Street NW
Washington, D.C. 20008
Tel: 202-332-9044
Fax: 202-332-9046
www.mewashingtondc.com

Embassy of the Republic of Namibia
1605 New Hampshire Avenue NW
Washington, D.C. 20009
Tel: 202-986-0540
Fax: 202-986-0443
www.namibianembassyusa.org

Royal Nepalese Embassy
2131 Leroy Place NW
Washington, D.C. 20008
Tel: 202-667-4550
Fax: 202-667-5534

Royal Netherlands Embassy
4200 Linnean Avenue NW
Washington, D.C. 20008
Tel: 202-244-5300
Fax: 202-362-3430
www.netherlands-embassy.org

New Zealand Embassy
37 Observatory Circle
Washington, D.C. 20008
Tel: 202-328-4800
Fax: 202-667-5227
www.nzemb.org

The Republic of Nicaragua
1627 New Hampshire Avenue NW
Washington, D.C. 20009
Tel: 202-939-6570
Fax: 202-939-6542

The Republic of Niger
2204 R Street NW
Washington, D.C. 20008
Tel: 202-483-4224
Fax: 202-483-3169
www.nigerembassyusa.org

The Federal Republic of Nigeria
1333 16th Street NW
Washington, D.C. 20036
Tel: 202-986-8400
Fax: 202-462-7124
www.nigeriaembassyusa.org

Royal Norwegian Embassy
2720 34th Street NW
Washington, D.C. 20008
Tel: 202-333-6000
Fax: 202-337-0870
www.norway.org

The Sultanate of Oman
2535 Belmont Road NW
Washington, D.C. 20008
Tel: 202-387-1980
Fax: 202-745-4933

The Islamic Republic of Pakistan
3517 International Court
Washington, D.C. 20008
Tel: 202-243-6500
Fax: 202-686-1534
www.embassyofpakistan.com

The Republic of Panama
2862 McGill Terrace NW
Washington, D.C. 20008
Tel: 202-483-1407
Fax: 202-483-8413
www.embassyofpanama.com

Embassy of Papua New Guinea
1779 Massachusetts Avenue NW
Suite 805
Washington, D.C. 20036
Tel: 202-745-3680
Fax: 202-745-3679
www.pngembassy.org

Paraguay
2400 Massachusetts Avenue NW
Washington, D.C. 20008
Tel: 202-483-6960
Fax: 202-234-4508

Embassy of Peru
1700 Massachusetts Avenue NW
Washington, D.C. 20036
Tel: 202-833-9860
Fax: 202-659-8124
www.peruvianembassy.us

Embassy of the Philippines

1600 Massachusetts Avenue NW
Washington, D.C. 20036
Tel: 202-467-9300
Fax: 202-467-9417
www.philippineembassy-usa.org

Embassy of Poland

2640 16th Street NW
Washington, D.C. 20009
Tel: 202-234-3800
Fax: 202-328-6271
www.polandembassy.org

Embassy of Portugal

2125 Kalorama Road NW
Washington, D.C. 20008
Tel: 202-328-8610
Fax: 202-462-3726
www.portugalemb.org

Embassy of The State of Qatar

2555 M Street NW
Washington, D.C. 20037
Tel: 202-274-1600
Fax: 202-237-0061
www.qatarembassy.net

Embassy of Romania

1607 23rd Street NW
Washington, D.C. 20008
Tel: 202-332-4848
Fax: 202-232-4748
www.roembus.org

Embassy of the Russian Federation

2650 Wisconsin Avenue NW
Washington, D.C. 20007
Tel: 202-298-5700
Fax: 202-298-5735
www.russianembassy.org

The Republic of Rwanda

1714 New Hampshire Avenue NW
Washington, D.C. 20009
Tel: 202-232-2882
Fax: 202-232-4544
www.rwandemb.org

Embassy of Saint Kitts and Nevis

3216 New Mexico Avenue NW
Washington, D.C. 20016
Tel: 202-686-2636
Fax: 202-686-5740

Embassy of Saint Lucia

3216 New Mexico Avenue NW
Washington, D.C. 20016
Tel: 202-364-6792 /93 /94 /95
Fax: 202-364-6723

Embassy of Saint Vincent and the Grenadines

3216 New Mexico Avenue NW
Washington, D.C. 20016
Tel: 202-364-6730
Fax: 202-364-6736

Royal Embassy of Saudi Arabia

601 New Hampshire Avenue NW
Washington, D.C. 20037
Tel: 202-342-3800
www.saudiembassy.net

Embassy of the Republic of Senegal

2112 Wyoming Avenue NW
Washington, D.C. 20008
Tel: 202-234-0540
Fax: 202-332-6315
www.senegalembassy-us.org

Embassy of Serbia and Montenegro

2134 Kalorama Road NW
Washington, D.C. 20008
Tel: 202-332-0333
Fax: 202-332-3933
www.serbiaembusa.org

Embassy of Sierra Leone
1701 19th Street NW
Washington, D.C. 20009
Tel: 202-939-9261
Fax: 202-483-1793

The Republic of Singapore
3501 International Place NW
Washington, D.C. 20008
Tel: 202-537-3100
Fax: 202-537-0876

Embassy of the Slovak Republic
3523 International Court NW
Washington, D.C. 20008
Tel: 202-237-1054
Fax: 202-237-6438
www.slovakembassy-us.org

Embassy of the Republic of Slovenia
1525 New Hampshire Avenue NW
Washington, D.C. 20036
Tel: 202-667-5363
Fax: 202-667-4563
www.mzz.gov.si/index.php?id=6&L=2

South African Embassy
3051 Massachusetts Avenue NW
Washington, D.C. 20008
Tel: 202-232-4400
Fax: 202-265-1607
www.saembassy.org

Embassy of Spain
2375 Pennsylvania Avenue NW
Washington, D.C. 20037
Tel: 202-452-0100
Fax: 202-833-5670
www.mae.es/en/home

Sri Lanka
2148 Wyoming Avenue NW
Washington, D.C. 20008
Tel: 202-483-4025 /26 /27 /28
Fax: 202-232-7181
www.slembassyusa.org

Embassy of the Republic of the Sudan
2210 Massachusetts Avenue NW
Washington, D.C. 20008
Tel: 202-338-8565
Fax: 202-667-2406
www.sudanembassy.org

Embassy of the Republic of Suriname
4301 Connecticut Avenue NW
Suite 460
Washington, D.C. 20008
Tel: 202-244-7488
Fax: 202-244-5878

Embassy of the Kingdom of Swaziland
3400 International Drive NW
Washington, D.C. 20008

Embassy of Sweden
2900 K Street
Washington, D.C. 20007
Tel: 202-467-2600
Fax: 202-467-2656
www.swedenabroad.se

Embassy of Switzerland
2900 Cathedral Avenue NW
Washington, D.C. 20008
Tel: 202-745-7900
Fax: 202-387-2564
www.swissemb.org

The Syrian Arab Republic
2215 Wyoming Avenue NW
Washington, D.C. 20008
Tel: 202-232-6313
Fax: 202-234-9548

The Republic of China on Taiwan
4201 Wisconsin Avenue NW
Washington, D.C. 20016
Tel: 202-895-1800
Fax: 202-966-0825

Embassy of Tajikistan
1005 New Hampshire Avenue NW
Washington, D.C. 20037
Tel: 202-223-6090
Fax: 202-223-6091
www.tjus.org

The United Republic of Tanzania
2139 R Street NW
Washington, D.C. 20008
Tel: 202-939-6125
Fax: 202-797-7408
www.tanzaniaembassy-us.org

Royal Thai Embassy
1024 Wisconsin Avenue NW
Suite 401
Washington, D.C. 20007
Tel: 202-944-3600
Fax: 202-944-3611
www.thaiembdc.org

The Republic of Togo
2208 Massachusetts Avenue NW
Washington, D.C. 20008
Tel: 202-234-4212
Fax: 202-232-3190

The Republic of Trinidad and Tobago
1708 Massachusetts Avenue NW
Washington, D.C. 20036
Tel: 202-467-6490
Fax: 202-785-3130
www.ttembassy.cjb.net

Tunisia
1515 Massachusetts Avenue NW
Washington, D.C. 20005
Tel: 202-862-1850
Fax: 202-862-1858

Embassy of the Republic of Turkey
2525 Massachusetts Avenue NW
Washington, D.C. 20008
Tel: 202-612-6700
Fax: 202-612-6744
www.turkishembassy.org

Embassy of Uganda
5911 16th Street NW
Washington, D.C. 20011
Tel: 202-726-7100
Fax: 202-726-1727
www.ugandaembassy.us

Embassy of Ukraine
3350 M Street NW
Washington, D.C. 20007
Tel: 202-333-0606
Fax: 202-333-0817
www.ukraineinfo.us

The United Arab Emirates
3522 International Court NW
Suite 400
Washington, D.C. 20008
Tel: 202-243-2400
Fax: 202-243-2432

The United Kingdom of Great Britain and Northern Ireland
3100 Massachusetts Avenue NW
Washington, D.C. 20006
Tel: 202-588-6500
Fax: 202-588-7870
www.britainusa.com/embassy

Embassy of Uruguay
1913 I Street NW
Washington D.C. 20006
Tel: 202-331-1313
Fax: 202-331-8142
www.uruwashi.org

Embassy of the Republic of Uzbekistan
1746 Massachusetts Avenue NW
Washington, D.C. 20036
Tel: 202-887-5300
Fax: 202-293-6804
www.uzbekistan.org

The Embassy of Venezuela
1099 30th Street NW
Washington, D.C. 20007
Tel: 202-342-2214
Fax: 202-342-6820
www.embavenez-us.org

The Embassy of Vietnam
1233 20th Street NW
Suite 400
Washington, D.C. 20037
Tel: 202-861-0737
Fax: 202-861-0917
www.vietnamembassy-usa.org

Embassy of the Independent State of Samoa
800 2nd Avenue
Suite 400D
New York, NY 10017
Tel: 212-599-6196
Fax: 212-599-0797

Embassy of Yemen
2319 Wyoming Avenue NW
Washington, D.C. 20037
Tel: 202-965-4760
Fax: 202-337-2017
www.yemenembassy.org

The Republic of Zambia
2419 Massachusetts Avenue NW
Washington, D.C. 20008
Tel: 202-265-9717
Fax: 202-332-0826

The Republic of Zimbabwe
1608 New Hampshire Avenue NW
Washington, D.C. 20009
Tel: 202-332-7100
Fax: 202-483-9326

Organizaciones y servicios públicos

Muchas bibliotecas y gobiernos estatales ofrecen cursos gratis para guiar a candidatos a través del proceso entero de naturalización—incluso preparación para el examen escrito. Pide a un oficial de la biblioteca más cercana. Además, hay muchas organizaciones nacionales y comunitarias que ayudan a candidatos con toda especie de servicio. Lo siguiente es una lista de tales organizaciones:

Asian-American Community Service Association
11322-F East 21st Street
Tulsa, OK 74129
Tel: 918-234-7431
Fax: 918-234-3148

Ayuda, Inc.
1736 Columbia Road, NW
Washington, D.C. 20009
Tel: 202-387-4848
Fax: 202-387-0324
www.ayudainc.org

American Immigration Lawyers Association
918 F Street, NW
Washington, D.C. 20004-1400
Tel: 202/216-2400
Fax: 202/371-9449
www.aila.org

Catholic Charities USA
1731 King Street, Suite 200 Alexandria, VA 22314
Tel: 703-549-1390
Fax: 703-549-1656
www.catholiccharitiesusa.org

Citizenship NYC
Tel: 888-374-5100
www.nyc.gov/html/dycd/html/cnyc.html

Colombian American Service Association (C.A.S.A.)
3138 Coral Way
Miami, FL 33145
Tel: 305-448-2272
Fax: 305-448-0178
www.casa-usa.org

Emerald Isle Immigration Center
Queens Office
59-26 Woodside Avenue
Woodside, NY 11377
Tel: 718-478-5502
Fax: 718-446-3727
Bronx Office
280 East 236th Street
Woodlawn, NY 10470
Tel: 718-324-3039
Fax: 718-324-7741
www.eiic.org

Ethiopian Community Development Council, Inc.
1038 South Highland Street
Arlington, VA 22204
Tel: 703-685-0510
Fax: 703-685-0529
www.ecdcinternational.org

The Hebrew Immigrant Aid Society
333 Seventh Avenue, 17th Floor
New York, NY 10001-5004
Tel: 212-967-4100
Fax: 212-967-4483
www.hias.org

Indo-American Center
6328 N. California Avenue
Chicago, IL 60659
Tel: 773-973-4444
Fax: 773-973-0157
www.indoamerican.org

Korean American Coalition
3421 W. 8th Street, 2nd Floor
Los Angeles, CA 90005
Tel: 213-365-5990
Fax: 213-380-7990
www.kac83.org

League of United Latin American Citizens Foundation (LULAC)
1601 Matamoros Street
P.O. Box 880
Laredo, TX 78042-0880
Tel: 956-722-5544
Fax: 956-722-7731
www.lulac.org

Los Angeles Unified School District Division of Adult and Career Education
P.O. Box 513307
Los Angeles, CA 90051
Tel: 213-625-3276
www.lausd.k12.ca.us

Lutheran Immigration and Refugee Service
(National Headquarters)
700 Light Street
Baltimore, MD 21230
Tel: 410-230-2700
Fax: 410-230-2890
www.lirs.org

Maryland Office for New Americans (MONA)
Department of Human Resources
311 W. Saratoga Street, Room 222
Baltimore, MD 21201
Tel: 410-767-7514
www.dhr.state.md.us/mona.htm

The Commonwealth of Massachusetts Office for Refugees and Immigrants
18 Tremont Street, Suite 600
Boston, MA 02108
Tel: 617-727-7888
Fax: 617-727-1822
TTY: 617-727-8149
www.state.ma.us/ori/ORI-homepage.html

Naturalization Services Program Department of Community Services and Development
P.O. Box 1947
Sacramento, CA 95814
Tel: 916-322-2940
Fax: 916- 319-5001
www.csd.ca.gov/Naturalization.htm

New Americans of Washington
615 Market Street, Suite G
Kirkland, WA 98052
Tel: 425-822-2523
Fax: 425-822-2592
www.newamericans.com

New York Association for New Americans, Inc.
17 Battery Place
New York, NY 10004-1102
Tel: 212-425-2900
www.nyana.org

Services, Immigrant Rights, and Education Network (SIREN)
778 North First Street, Suite 202
San Jose, CA 95112
Tel: 408-286-5680, x104
Vietnamese Q&A: 408-286-1448
www.siren-bayarea.org

St. Anselm's Cross-Cultural Community Center
13091 Galway Street
Garden Grove, CA 92844
Tel: 714-537-0608
Fax: 714-537-7606
www.saintanselmgg.org

Office of Migration & Refugee Services United States Conference of Catholic Bishops
3211 4th Street, N.E.
Washington, D.C. 20017-1194
Tel: 202-541-3000
www.nccbuscc.org

Para más sitios de Web, busca en www.google.com las frases "naturalization assistance", "citizenship assistance", "naturalization programs" o
"citizenship programs", junto con el nombre de la ciudad o el estado
donde vives.

Formularios necesarios USCIS

Los siguientes formularios USCIS y las instrucciones son copias idénticas de unas solicitudes que tendrías que presentar durante el proceso de naturalización. Estos no se pueden usar oficialmente, pero son útiles para familiarizarte con el diseño y lo que tendrías que rellenar. Para conseguir los formularios oficiales, los puedes cargar gratis de www.uscis.gov o puedes llamar al USCIS Customer Service Line a 1-800-375-5283. Es importante tener presente que USCIS de vez en cuando aumenta el honorario de presentación de estos documentos; hay que confirmar todos los honorarios antes de enviar la solicitud.

Form N-400	*Application for Naturalization*
Form N-426	*Request for Certification of Military or Naval Service*
Form N-600	*Application for Certificate of Citizenship*
Form I-130	*Petition for Alien Relative*
Form I-131	*Application for Travel Document*
Form I-140	*Immigrant Petition for Alien Worker*
	(El formulario se presenta en nombre de un extranjero)
Form I-485	*Application to Register Permanent Residence or Adjust Status*
Form I-539	*Application to Extend/Change Nonimmigrant Status*

New Photo Standards

OMB No. 1615-0052; Expires 10/31/08

Department of Homeland Security
U.S Citizenship and Immigration Services

N-400 Application
for Naturalization

Print clearly or type your answers using CAPITAL letters. Failure to print clearly may delay your application. Use black ink.

Part 1. Your Name. *(The person applying for naturalization.)*

A. Your current legal name.

Family Name *(Last Name)*

Given Name *(First Name)*　　　　Full Middle Name *(If applicable)*

B. Your name **exactly** as it appears on your Permanent Resident Card.

Family Name *(Last Name)*

Given Name *(First Name)*　　　　Full Middle Name *(If applicable)*

C. If you have ever used other names, provide them below.

Family Name *(Last Name)*	Given Name *(First Name)*	Middle Name

D. Name change *(optional)*

Please read the Instructions before you decide whether to change your name.

1. Would you like to legally change your name?　☐ Yes　☐ No

2. If "Yes," print the new name you would like to use. Do not use initials or abbreviations when writing your new name.

Family Name *(Last Name)*

Given Name *(First Name)*　　　　Full Middle Name

Part 2. Information about your eligibility. *(Check only one.)*

I am at least 18 years old **AND**

A. ☐ I have been a Lawful Permanent Resident of the United States for at least five years.

B. ☐ I have been a Lawful Permanent Resident of the United States for at least three years, **and** I have been married to and living with the same U.S. citizen for the last three years, **and** my spouse has been a U.S. citizen for the last three years.

C. ☐ I am applying on the basis of qualifying military service.

D. ☐ Other *(Please explain)* _____

Write your USCIS "A"- number here:
A

For USCIS Use Only

Bar Code	Date Stamp

Remarks

Action Block

A. U.S. Social Security Number   **B.** Date of Birth *(mm/dd/yyyy)*   **C.** Date You Became a Permanent Resident *(mm/dd/yyyy)*

D. Country of Birth   **E.** Country of Nationality

F. Are either of your parents U.S. citizens? *(If yes, see instructions.)*   ☐ Yes   ☐ No

G. What is your current marital status?   ☐ Single, Never Married   ☐ Married   ☐ Divorced   ☐ Widowed

☐ Marriage Annulled or Other *(Explain)* _____

H. Are you requesting a waiver of the English and/or U.S. History and Government
requirements based on a disability or impairment and attaching a Form N-648 with   ☐ Yes   ☐ No
your application?

I. Are you requesting an accommodation to the naturalization process because of a
disability or impairment? *(See Instructions for some examples of accommodations.)*   ☐ Yes   ☐ No

If you answered "Yes," check the box below that applies:

☐ I am deaf or hearing impaired and need a sign language interpreter who uses the following language: _____

☐ I use a wheelchair.

☐ I am blind or sight impaired.

☐ I will need another type of accommodation. Please explain: _____

_____

_____

Part 4. Addresses and telephone numbers.

A. Home Address - Street Number and Name *(Do **not** write a P.O. Box in this space.)*   Apartment Number

City	County	State	ZIP Code	Country

B. Care of   Mailing Address - Street Number and Name *(If different from home address)*   Apartment Number

City	State	ZIP Code	Country

C. Daytime Phone Number *(If any)*   Evening Phone Number *(If any)*   E-mail Address *(If any)*

(   )   (   )

Part 5. Information for criminal records search.	Write your USCIS "A"- number here: A

NOTE: The categories below are those required by the FBI. See Instructions for more information.

A. Gender

☐ Male   ☐ Female

B. Height

Feet	Inches

C. Weight

Pounds

D. Are you Hispanic or Latino?   ☐ Yes   ☐ No

E. Race *(Select one or more.)*

☐ White   ☐ Asian   ☐ Black or African American   ☐ American Indian or Alaskan Native   ☐ Native Hawaiian or Other Pacific Islander

F. Hair color

☐ Black   ☐ Brown   ☐ Blonde   ☐ Gray   ☐ White   ☐ Red   ☐ Sandy   ☐ Bald (No Hair)

G. Eye color

☐ Brown   ☐ Blue   ☐ Green   ☐ Hazel   ☐ Gray   ☐ Black   ☐ Pink   ☐ Maroon   ☐ Other

Part 6. Information about your residence and employment.

A. Where have you lived during the last five years? Begin with where you live now and then list every place you lived for the last five years. If you need more space, use a separate sheet(s) of paper.

Street Number and Name, Apartment Number, City, State, Zip Code and Country	Dates *(mm/dd/yyyy)*	
	From	To
Current Home Address - Same as Part 4.A		Present

B. Where have you worked (or, if you were a student, what schools did you attend) during the last five years? Include military service. Begin with your current or latest employer and then list every place you have worked or studied for the last five years. If you need more space, use a separate sheet of paper.

Employer or School Name	Employer or School Address *(Street, City and State)*	Dates *(mm/dd/yyyy)*		Your Occupation
		From	To	

Part 7. Time outside the United States.
(Including Trips to Canada, Mexico and the Caribbean Islands)

A. How many total days did you spend outside of the United States during the past five years? ☐ days

B. How many trips of 24 hours or more have you taken outside of the United States during the past five years? ☐ trips

C. List below all the trips of 24 hours or more that you have taken outside of the United States since becoming a Lawful Permanent Resident. Begin with your most recent trip. If you need more space, use a separate sheet(s) of paper.

Date You Left the United States *(mm/dd/yyyy)*	Date You Returned to the United States *(mm/dd/yyyy)*	Did Trip Last Six Months or More?	Countries to Which You Traveled	Total Days Out of the United States
		☐ Yes ☐ No		
		☐ Yes ☐ No		
		☐ Yes ☐ No		
		☐ Yes ☐ No		
		☐ Yes ☐ No		
		☐ Yes ☐ No		
		☐ Yes ☐ No		
		☐ Yes ☐ No		
		☐ Yes ☐ No		
		☐ Yes ☐ No		

Part 8. Information about your marital history.

A. How many times have you been married (including annulled marriages)? ☐ If you have **never** been married, go to Part 9.

B. If you are now married, give the following information about your spouse:

1. Spouse's Family Name *(Last Name)*   Given Name *(First Name)*   Full Middle Name *(If applicable)*

2. Date of Birth *(mm/dd/yyyy)*   **3.** Date of Marriage *(mm/dd/yyyy)*   **4.** Spouse's U.S. Social Security #

5. Home Address - Street Number and Name   Apartment Number

City   State   Zip Code

C. Is your spouse a U.S. citizen?   ☐ Yes   ☐ No

D. If your spouse is a U.S. citizen, give the following information:

1. When did your spouse become a U.S. citizen?   ☐ At Birth   ☐ Other

If "Other," give the following information:

2. Date your spouse became a U.S. citizen

3. Place your spouse became a U.S. citizen *(Please see Instructions.)*

City and State

E. If your spouse is **not** a U.S. citizen, give the following information :

1. Spouse's Country of Citizenship

2. Spouse's USCIS "A"- Number *(If applicable)*

A

3. Spouse's Immigration Status

☐ Lawful Permanent Resident   ☐ Other

F. If you were married before, provide the following information about your prior spouse. If you have more than one previous marriage, use a separate sheet(s) of paper to provide the information requested in Questions 1-5 below.

1. Prior Spouse's Family Name *(Last Name)*   Given Name *(First Name)*   Full Middle Name *(If applicable)*

2. Prior Spouse's Immigration Status
☐ U.S. Citizen
☐ Lawful Permanent Resident
☐ Other

3. Date of Marriage *(mm/dd/yyyy)*

4. Date Marriage Ended *(mm/dd/yyyy)*

5. How Marriage Ended
☐ Divorce   ☐ Spouse Died   ☐ Other

G. How many times has your current spouse been married (including annulled marriages)?

If your spouse has **ever** been married before, give the following information about **your spouse's** prior marriage.
If your spouse has more than one previous marriage, use a separate sheet(s) of paper to provide the information requested in Questions 1 - 5 below.

1. Prior Spouse's Family Name *(Last Name)*   Given Name *(First Name)*   Full Middle Name *(If applicable)*

2. Prior Spouse's Immigration Status
☐ U.S. Citizen
☐ Lawful Permanent Resident
☐ Other

3. Date of Marriage *(mm/dd/yyyy)*

4. Date Marriage Ended *(mm/dd/yyyy)*

5. How Marriage Ended
☐ Divorce   ☐ Spouse Died   ☐ Other

Part 9. Information about your children.	Write your USCIS "A"- number here: A

A. How many sons and daughters have you had? For more information on which sons and daughters you should include and how to complete this section, see the Instructions.

B. Provide the following information about all of your sons and daughters. If you need more space, use a separate sheet(s) of paper.

Full Name of Son or Daughter	Date of Birth (mm/dd/yyyy)	USCIS "A"- number (if child has one)	Country of Birth	Current Address (Street, City, State and Country)
		A		
		A		
		A		
		A		
		A		
		A		
		A		
		A		

Add Children | Go to continuation page

Part 10. Additional questions.

Please answer Questions 1 through 14. If you answer "Yes" to any of these questions, include a written explanation with this form. Your written explanation should (1) explain why your answer was "Yes" and (2) provide any additional information that helps to explain your answer.

A. General Questions.

1. Have you **ever** claimed to be a U.S. citizen *(in writing or any other way)*? ☐ Yes ☐ No

2. Have you **ever** registered to vote in any Federal, state or local election in the United States? ☐ Yes ☐ No

3. Have you **ever** voted in any Federal, state or local election in the United States? ☐ Yes ☐ No

4. Since becoming a Lawful Permanent Resident, have you **ever** failed to file a required Federal state or local tax return? ☐ Yes ☐ No

5. Do you owe any Federal, state or local taxes that are overdue? ☐ Yes ☐ No

6. Do you have any title of nobility in any foreign country? ☐ Yes ☐ No

7. Have you ever been declared legally incompetent or been confined to a mental institution within the last five years? ☐ Yes ☐ No

B. Affiliations.

8. a Have you **ever** been a member of or associated with any organization, association, fund foundation, party, club, society or similar group in the United States or in any other place? ☐ Yes ☐ No

b. If you answered "Yes," list the name of each group below. If you need more space, attach the names of the other group(s) on a separate sheet(s) of paper.

Name of Group		Name of Group	
1.		6.	
2.		7.	
3.		8.	
4.		9.	
5.		10.	

9. Have you **ever** been a member of or in any way associated *(either directly or indirectly)* with:

a. The Communist Party? ☐ Yes ☐ No

b. Any other totalitarian party? ☐ Yes ☐ No

c. A terrorist organization? ☐ Yes ☐ No

10. Have you **ever** advocated *(either directly or indirectly)* the overthrow of any government by force or violence? ☐ Yes ☐ No

11. Have you **ever** persecuted *(either directly or indirectly)* any person because of race, religion, national origin, membership in a particular social group or political opinion? ☐ Yes ☐ No

12. Between March 23, 1933 and May 8, 1945, did you work for or associate in any way *(either directly or indirectly)* with:

a. The Nazi government of Germany? ☐ Yes ☐ No

b. Any government in any area (1) occupied by, (2) allied with, or (3) established with the help of the Nazi government of Germany? ☐ Yes ☐ No

c. Any German, Nazi, or S.S. military unit, paramilitary unit, self-defense unit, vigilante unit, citizen unit, police unit, government agency or office, extermination camp, concentration camp, prisoner of war camp, prison, labor camp or transit camp? ☐ Yes ☐ No

C. Continuous Residence.

Since becoming a Lawful Permanent Resident of the United States:

13. Have you **ever** called yourself a "nonresident" on a Federal, state or local tax return? ☐ Yes ☐ No

14. Have you **ever** failed to file a Federal, state or local tax return because you considered yourself to be a "nonresident"? ☐ Yes ☐ No

D. Good Moral Character.

For the purposes of this application, you must answer "Yes" to the following questions, if applicable, even if your records were sealed or otherwise cleared or if anyone, including a judge, law enforcement officer or attorney, told you that you no longer have a record.

15. Have you **ever** committed a crime or offense for which you were **not** arrested?   ☐ Yes ☐ No

16. Have you **ever** been arrested, cited or detained by any law enforcement officer
(including USCIS or former INS and military officers) for any reason?   ☐ Yes ☐ No

17. Have you **ever** been charged with committing any crime or offense?   ☐ Yes ☐ No

18. Have you **ever** been convicted of a crime or offense?   ☐ Yes ☐ No

19. Have you **ever** been placed in an alternative sentencing or a rehabilitative program
(for example: diversion, deferred prosecution, withheld adjudication, deferred adjudication)?   ☐ Yes ☐ No

20. Have you **ever** received a suspended sentence, been placed on probation or been paroled?   ☐ Yes ☐ No

21. Have you **ever** been in jail or prison?   ☐ Yes ☐ No

If you answered "Yes" to any of Questions 15 through 21, complete the following table. If you need more space, use a separate sheet (s) of paper to give the same information.

Why were you arrested, cited, detained or charged?	Date arrested, cited, detained or charged? *(mm/dd/yyyy)*	Where were you arrested, cited, detained or charged? *(City, State, Country)*	Outcome or disposition of the arrest, citation, detention or charge *(No charges filed, charges dismissed, jail, probation, etc.)*

Answer Questions 22 through 33. If you answer "Yes" to any of these questions, attach (1) your written explanation why your answer was "Yes" and (2) any additional information or documentation that helps explain your answer.

22. Have you **ever**:

    a. Been a habitual drunkard?   ☐ Yes ☐ No

    b. Been a prostitute, or procured anyone for prostitution?   ☐ Yes ☐ No

    c. Sold or smuggled controlled substances, illegal drugs or narcotics?   ☐ Yes ☐ No

    d. Been married to more than one person at the same time?   ☐ Yes ☐ No

    e. Helped anyone enter or try to enter the United States illegally?   ☐ Yes ☐ No

    f. Gambled illegally or received income from illegal gambling?   ☐ Yes ☐ No

    g. Failed to support your dependents or to pay alimony?   ☐ Yes ☐ No

23. Have you **ever** given false or misleading information to any U.S. government official
while applying for any immigration benefit or to prevent deportation, exclusion or removal?   ☐ Yes ☐ No

24. Have you **ever** lied to any U.S. government official to gain entry or admission into the
United States?   ☐ Yes ☐ No

E. Removal, Exclusion and Deportation Proceedings.

25. Are removal, exclusion, rescission or deportation proceedings pending against you? ☐ Yes ☐ No

26. Have you **ever** been removed, excluded or deported from the United States? ☐ Yes ☐ No

27. Have you **ever** been ordered to be removed, excluded or deported from the United States? ☐ Yes ☐ No

28. Have you **ever** applied for any kind of relief from removal, exclusion or deportation? ☐ Yes ☐ No

F. Military Service.

29. Have you **ever** served in the U.S. Armed Forces? ☐ Yes ☐ No

30. Have you **ever** left the United States to avoid being drafted into the U.S. Armed Forces? ☐ Yes ☐ No

31. Have you **ever** applied for any kind of exemption from military service in the U.S. Armed Forces? ☐ Yes ☐ No

32. Have you **ever** deserted from the U.S. Armed Forces? ☐ Yes ☐ No

G. Selective Service Registration.

33. Are you a male who lived in the United States at any time between your 18th and 26th birthdays ☐ Yes ☐ No
in any status except as a lawful nonimmigrant?

If you answered "NO," go on to question 34.

If you answered "YES," provide the information below.

If you answered "YES," but you did not register with the Selective Service System and are still under 26 years of age, you must register before you apply for naturalization, so that you can complete the information below:

Date Registered (mm/dd/yyyy) [   ] Selective Service Number [   ]

If you answered "YES," but you did not register with the Selective Service and you are now 26 years old or older, attach a statement explaining why you did not register.

H. Oath Requirements. *(See Part 14 for the Text of the Oath.)*

Answer Questions 34 through 39. If you answer "No" to any of these questions, attach (1) your written explanation why the answer was "No" and (2) any additional information or documentation that helps to explain your answer.

34. Do you support the Constitution and form of government of the United States? ☐ Yes ☐ No

35. Do you understand the full Oath of Allegiance to the United States? ☐ Yes ☐ No

36. Are you willing to take the full Oath of Allegiance to the United States? ☐ Yes ☐ No

37. If the law requires it, are you willing to bear arms on behalf of the United States? ☐ Yes ☐ No

38. If the law requires it, are you willing to perform noncombatant services in the U.S. Armed Forces? ☐ Yes ☐ No

39. If the law requires it, are you willing to perform work of national importance under civilian ☐ Yes ☐ No
direction?

Part 11. Your signature.

Write your USCIS "A"- number here:
A

I certify, under penalty of perjury under the laws of the United States of America, that this application, and the evidence submitted with it, are all true and correct. I authorize the release of any information that the USCIS needs to determine my eligibility for naturalization.

Your Signature

Date *(mm/dd/yyyy)*

Part 12. Signature of person who prepared this application for you. *(If applicable.)*

I declare under penalty of perjury that I prepared this application at the request of the above person. The answers provided are based on information of which I have personal knowledge and/or were provided to me by the above named person in response to the *exact questions* contained on this form.

Preparer's Printed Name

Preparer's Signature

Date *(mm/dd/yyyy)*

Preparer's Firm or Organization Name *(If applicable)*

Preparer's Daytime Phone Number

Preparer's Address - Street Number and Name

City

State

Zip Code

NOTE: Do not complete Parts 13 and 14 until a USCIS Officer instructs you to do so.

Part 13. Signature at interview.

I swear (affirm) and certify under penalty of perjury under the laws of the United States of America that I know that the contents of this application for naturalization subscribed by me, including corrections numbered 1 through _____ and the evidence submitted by me numbered pages 1 through _____ , are true and correct to the best of my knowledge and belief.

Subscribed to and sworn to (affirmed) before me

Officer's Printed Name or Stamp

Date *(mm/dd/yyyy)*

Complete Signature of Applicant

Officer's Signature

Part 14. Oath of Allegiance.

If your application is approved, you will be scheduled for a public oath ceremony at which time you will be required to take the following oath of allegiance immediately prior to becoming a naturalized citizen. By signing, you acknowledge your willingness and ability to take this oath:

I hereby declare, on oath, that I absolutely and entirely renounce and abjure all allegiance and fidelity to any foreign prince, potentate, state, or sovereignty, of whom or which I have heretofore been a subject or citizen;

that I will support and defend the Constitution and laws of the United States of America against all enemies, foreign and domestic;

that I will bear true faith and allegiance to the same;

that I will bear arms on behalf of the United States when required by the law;

that I will perform noncombatant service in the Armed Forces of the United States when required by the law;

that I will perform work of national importance under civilian direction when required by the law; and

that I take this obligation freely, without any mental reservation or purpose of evasion; so help me God.

Printed Name of Applicant

Complete Signature of Applicant

Department of Homeland Security
U.S. Citizenship and Immigration Services

N-426, Request for Certification of Military or Naval Service

Instructions

(Please discard this sheet before submitting request. Submit in triplicate, that is, all six pages of the form.)

NOTE: Please type or print in block letters with a ball-point pen, using black ink. Be sure this form and the complete return address are legible. Do not leave any questions unanswered. When appropriate insert "none," "not applicable" or "N/A."

What Is the Purpose of This Form?

The principal purpose of this form is to solicit information to secure a duly authenticated certification of honorable active duty service from the U.S. Government Executive Department, under which you served or are serving, to satisfy statutory requirements for naturalization as a U.S. citizen.

Submission of the information is voluntary. If your U.S. Social Security number requested on the form is not provided, no right, benefit or privilege will be denied for such failure. However, as military records are indexed by such numbers, verification of your military service may prove difficult.

If you are applying for naturalization under Sections 328 or 329 of the Immigration and Nationality Act, you should submit this form and Form G-325B, Biographic Information, with your Form N-400, Application for Naturalization, to U.S. Citizenship and Immigration Services (USCIS).

What Is Our Authority for Collecting This Information?

Our authority for collecting the information requested on this form is contained in Sections 328 and 329 of the Immigration and Nationality Act of 1952 (8 U.S.C. 1439 and 1440).

All or part of the information solicited may as a matter of routine use be disclosed to courts exercising naturalization jurisdiction and to other Federal, state, local and foreign law enforcement and regulatory agencies, the Department of Defense, including any component thereof, Selective Service System, Department of State, Department of the Treasury, Central Intelligence Agency, Interpol and individuals and organizations that process the application for naturalization, or during the courses of investigation, to elicit further information required by USCIS to carry out its functions.

Information solicited that indicates a violation or potential violation of law, whether civil, criminal or regulatory in nature, may be referred as a routine use to the appropriate agency, whether Federal, state, local or foreign, charged with the responsibility of investigating, enforcing or prosecuting such violations.

Failure to provide any or all of the solicited information may delay the naturalization process or result in a failure to locate military records or prove qualifying military service.

Paperwork Reduction Act Notice.

An agency may not conduct or sponsor an information collection and a person is not required to respond to a collection of information unless it displays a currently valid OMB control number.

This collection of information is estimated to average 45 minutes per response, including the time for reviewing instructions, searching existing data sources, gathering and maintaining the data needed, and completing and reviewing the collection of information.

Send comments regarding this burden estimate or any other aspect of this collection of information, including suggestions for reducing this burden to U.S. Citizenship and Immigration Services, Regulatory Management Division, 111 Massachusetts Avenue, N.W., 3rd Floor, Suite 3008 Washington, D.C. 20529. **Do not mail your completed application to this address.**

Department of Homeland Security
U.S. Citizenship and Immigration Services

N-426, Request for Certification of Military or Naval Service

Alien Registration Number	Date of Request

NOTE TO CERTIFYING OFFICER: For use in connection with my application for naturalization, please complete the certification of military service on **Pages 2, 4, and 6** of this form and furnish it to the office of U.S. Citizenship and Immigration Services (USCIS) shown in the address block below. The information shown below is furnished to help locate and identify my military records. **(Submit in triplicate, that is, all six pages of this form.)**

NOTE TO APPLICANT: Furnish as much information as possible. If you were issued a Report of Separation, DD Form 214, attach a copy. Fill in the blanks only on Pages 1, 3 and 5 of this form. Please type or print clearly in black ink. All copies must be legible. Do not use pencil. **(Submit in triplicate, that is, all six pages of this form.)**

Name Used During Active Service *(Last, First, Middle)*	U.S. Social Security Number	Date of Birth	Place of Birth

For an effective records search, it is important that ALL periods of service be shown below. (Use blank sheet(s) if more space is needed.)
Active Service:

Branch of Service *(Show also last organization, if known.)*	Date Entered on Active Duty	Date Released From Active Duty	Check Which Officer	Check Which Enlisted	Service Number During This Period
			☐	☐	
			☐	☐	
			☐	☐	
			☐	☐	

Reserve or National Guard Service: If none, check ☐ None

Branch of Service	Reserve	N. Guard	Date Membership Began	Date Membership Ended	Officer	Enlisted	Service Number During This Period
	☐	☐			☐	☐	
	☐	☐			☐	☐	
	☐	☐			☐	☐	

Check Which (Reserve / N. Guard)   *Check Which* (Officer / Enlisted)

Are you a Military Retiree or Fleet Reservist?   ☐ No   ☐ Yes

Signature *(Present Name)*	Present Address *(Number, Street, City, State and Zip Code)*

Instructions to Certifying Officer.

Persons who are serving or have served honorably under specified conditions in the armed forces of the United States, inclusive of the reserve components of the armed forces of the United States, are granted certain exemptions from the general requirements for naturalization. The law requires such service to be established by a duly authenticated copy of the records of the executive department having custody of the record of service, showing whether the service man or woman served honorably in an active-duty status, reserve-duty status, or both, and whether each separation from the service was under honorable conditions. For that purpose, the certified statement on **Pages 2, 4 and 6** of this form, executed under the seal of your department, is required and should cover not only the period(s) of service shown above, but any other periods of service (active, reserve or both) rendered by the service man or woman.

Pages 2, 4 and 6 of this form should be completed, or the information called for furnished by separate letter, and the form and letter returned to the office of U. S. Citizenship and Immigration Services at the address in the block immediately below.

U.S. Citizenship and Immigration Services

◄ **Return to:**
Please type
or print
complete
return
address.
Include zip
code.

Certification of Military or Naval Service.

☐ Name correctly shown on front of form.

☐ Name as shown in records:

Active Service.

1. Entered Service at	2. On	3. Served to	4. Branch of Service	5. State whether serving honorably. If separated, state whether under honorable conditions. If other than honorable, give full details. Always complete item 11.

Reserve or National Guard Service.

6. Branch of Service	7. Check Which		8. Began	9. Ended	10. State whether serving honorably. State if Selected Reserve of the Ready Reserve. If separated, state whether under honorable conditions. If other than honorable, give full details. Always complete Item 11.
	Reserve	N. Guard			
	☐	☐			
	☐	☐			

11. Statement Regarding Alienage. *(Complete this item in ALL cases.)*

☐ Record shows this person **was not** discharged on account of alienage.

☐ Record shows this person **was** discharged on account of alienage. Details: _____

12. Remarks. Use for continuation of any of the above items. You should also show in the space below any **derogatory information** in your records relating to the person's character, loyalty to the United States, disciplinary actions, convictions or other matters concerning his or her fitness for citizenship.

Lodge Act Enlistee.

Complete this block if subject is a "Lodge Act Enlistee"-64 Stat. 316 (Army). Subsequent to enlistment under the Lodge Act on _____

subject entered _____ at the port of _____

(the United States, American Samoa, Swains Island or the Panama Canal Zone)

pursuant to Military orders on _____ via _____

I CERTIFY that the information here given concerning the service of the person named on the face of this form is correct according to the records

of the _____

(Name of department or organization)

[SEAL]   **(Official Signature)** _____

Date _____ , _____   By _____

OMB No. 1615-0053; Expires 08/31/08

Department of Homeland Security
U.S. Citizenship and Immigration Services

N-426, Request for Certification of Military or Naval Service

Alien Registration Number		Date of Request

NOTE TO CERTIFYING OFFICER: For use in connection with my application for naturalization, please complete the certification of military service on **Pages 2, 4, and 6** of this form and furnish it to the office of U.S. Citizenship and Immigration Services (USCIS) shown in the address block below. The information shown below is furnished to help locate and identify my military records. **(Submit in triplicate, that is, all six pages of this form.)**

NOTE TO APPLICANT: Furnish as much information as possible. If you were issued a Report of Separation, DD Form 214, attach a copy. Fill in the blanks only on Pages 1, 3 and 5 of this form. Please type or print clearly in black ink. All copies must be legible. Do not use pencil. (Submit in triplicate, that is, all six pages of this form.)

Name Used During Active Service *(Last, First, Middle)*	U.S. Social Security Number	Date of Birth	Place of Birth

For an effective records search, it is important that ALL periods of service be shown below. (Use blank sheet(s) if more space is needed.)
Active Service:

Branch of Service *(Show also last organization, if known.)*	Date Entered on Active Duty	Date Released From Active Duty	Check Which		Service Number During This Period
			Officer	Enlisted	
			☐	☐	
			☐	☐	
			☐	☐	
			☐	☐	

Reserve or National Guard Service: If none, check ☐ None

Branch of Service	Check Which		Date Membership Began	Date Membership Ended	Check Which		Service Number During This Period
	Reserve	N. Guard			Officer	Enlisted	
	☐	☐			☐	☐	
	☐	☐			☐	☐	
	☐	☐			☐	☐	

Are you a Military Retiree or Fleet Reservist?	☐ No	☐ Yes

Signature *(Present Name)*	Present Address *(Number, Street, City, State and Zip Code)*

Instructions to Certifying Officer.

Persons who are serving or have served honorably under specified conditions in the armed forces of the United States, inclusive of the reserve components of the armed forces of the United States, are granted certain exemptions from the general requirements for naturalization. The law requires such service to be established by a duly authenticated copy of the records of the executive department having custody of the record of service, showing whether the service man or woman served honorably in an active-duty status, reserve-duty status, or both, and whether each separation from the service was under honorable conditions. For that purpose, the certified statement on **Pages 2, 4 and 6** of this form, executed under the seal of your department, is required and should cover not only the period(s) of service shown above, but any other periods of service (active, reserve or both) rendered by the service man or woman.

Pages 2, 4 and 6 of this form should be completed, or the information called for furnished by separate letter, and the form and letter returned to the office of U. S. Citizenship and Immigration Services at the address in the block immediately below.

U.S. Citizenship and Immigration Services

◀ **Return to:**

Please type
or print
complete
return
address.
Include zip
code.

Applicant: Do not fill out this page.

Certification of Military or Naval Service.

☐ Name correctly shown on front of form.

☐ Name as shown in records:

Active Service.

1. Entered Service at	2. On	3. Served to	4. Branch of Service	5. State whether serving honorably. If separated, state whether under honorable conditions. If other than honorable, give full details. Always complete item 11.

Reserve or National Guard Service.

6. Branch of Service	7. Check Which		8. Began	9. Ended	10. State whether serving honorably. State if Selected Reserve of the Ready Reserve. If separated, state whether under honorable conditions. If other than honorable, give full details. Always complete Item 11.
	Reserve	N. Guard			
	☐	☐			
	☐	☐			

11. **Statement Regarding Alienage.** *(Complete this item in ALL cases.)*

☐ Record shows this person **was not** discharged on account of alienage.

☐ Record shows this person **was** discharged on account of alienage. Details: _____

12. **Remarks.** Use for continuation of any of the above items. You should also show in the space below any **derogatory information** in your records relating to the person's character, loyalty to the United States, disciplinary actions, convictions or other matters concerning his or her fitness for citizenship.

Lodge Act Enlistee.

Complete this block if subject is a "Lodge Act Enlistee"-64 Stat. 316 (Army). Subsequent to enlistment under the Lodge Act on _____

subject entered _____ at the port of _____
(the United States, American Samoa, Swains Island or the Panama Canal Zone)

pursuant to Military orders on _____ via _____

I CERTIFY that the information here given concerning the service of the person named on the face of this form is correct according to the records

of the _____
(Name of department or organization)

[SEAL]   **(Official Signature)** _____

Date _____ , _____   By _____

OMB No. 1615-0053; Expires 08/31/08

Department of Homeland Security
U.S. Citizenship and Immigration Services

N-426, Request for Certification
of Military or Naval Service

Alien Registration Nu mber	Date of Request

NOTE TO CERTIFYING OFFICER: For use in connection with my application for naturalization, please complete the certification of military service on **Pages 2, 4, and 6** of this form and furnish it to the office of U.S. Citizenship and Immigration Services (USCIS) shown in the address block below. The information shown below is furnished to help locate and identify my military records. **(Submit in triplicate, that is, all six pages of this form.)**

NOTE TO APPLICANT: Furnish as much information as possible. If you were issued a Report of Separation, DD Form 214, attach a copy. Fill in the blanks only on Pages 1, 3 and 5 of this form. **Please type or print clearly in black ink. All copies must be legible. Do not use pencil. (Submit in triplicate, that is, all six pages of this form.)**

Name Used During Active Service *(Last, First, Middle)*	U.S. Social Security Number	Date of Birth	Place of Birth

For an effective records search, it is important that ALL periods of service be shown below. (Use blank sheet(s) if more space is needed.)
Active Service:

Branch of Service *(Show also last organization, if known.)*	Date Entered on Active Duty	Date Released From Active Duty	Check Which		Service Number During This Period
			Officer	Enlisted	
			☐	☐	
			☐	☐	
			☐	☐	
			☐	☐	

Reserve or National Guard Service: If none, check ☐ None

Branch of Service	Check Which		Date Membership Began	Date Membership Ended	Check Which		Service Number During This Period
	Reserve	N. Guard			Officer	Enlisted	
	☐	☐			☐	☐	
	☐	☐			☐	☐	
	☐	☐			☐	☐	

Are you a Military Retiree or Fleet Reservist?   ☐ No   ☐ Yes

Signature *(Present Name)*	Present Address *(Number, Street, City, State and Zip Code)*

Instructions to Certifying Officer.

Persons who are serving or have served honorably under specified conditions in the armed forces of the United States, inclusive of the reserve components of the armed forces of the United States, are granted certain exemptions from the general requirements for naturalization. The law requires such service to be established by a duly authenticated copy of the records of the executive department having custody of the record of service, showing whether the service man or woman served honorably in an active-duty status, reserve-duty status, or both, and whether each separation from the service was under honorable conditions. For that purpose, the certified statement on **Pages 2, 4, and 6** of this form, executed under the seal of your department, is required and should cover not only the period(s) of service shown above, but any other periods of service (active, reserve or both) rendered by the service man or woman.

Pages 2, 4 and 6 of this form should be completed, or the information called for furnished by separate letter, and the form and letter returned to the office of U. S. Citizenship and Immigration Services at the address in the block immediately below.

U.S. Citizenship and Immigration Services

◀ **Return to:**
Please type or print complete return address. Include zip code.

Certification of Military or Naval Service.

☐ Name correctly shown on front of form.

☐ Name as shown in records:

Active Service.

1. Entered Service at	2. On	3. Served to	4. Branch of Service	5. State whether serving honorably. If separated, state whether under honorable conditions. If other than honorable, give full details. Always complete item 11.

Reserve or National Guard Service.

6. Branch of Service	7. Check Which		8. Began	9. Ended	10. State whether serving honorably. State if Selected Reserve of the Ready Reserve. If separated, state whether under honorable conditions. If other than honorable, give full details. Always complete Item 11.
	Reserve	N. Guard			
	☐	☐			
	☐	☐			

11. Statement Regarding Alienage. *(Complete this item in ALL cases.)*

☐ Record shows this person **was not** discharged on account of alienage.

☐ Record shows this person **was** discharged on account of alienage. Details: _____

12. Remarks. Use for continuation of any of the above items. You should also show in the space below any **derogatory information** in your records relating to the person's character, loyalty to the United States, disciplinary actions, convictions or other matters concerning his or her fitness for citizenship.

Lodge Act Enlistee.

Complete this block if subject is a "Lodge Act Enlistee"-64 Stat. 316 (Army). Subsequent to enlistment under the Lodge Act on _____

subject entered _____ at the port of _____

(the United States, American Samoa, Swains Island or the Panama Canal Zone)

pursuant to Military orders on _____ via _____

I CERTIFY that the information here given concerning the service of the person named on the face of this form is correct according to the records

of the _____

(Name of department or organization)

[SEAL] **(Official Signature)** _____

Date _____ , _____ By _____

OMB No. 1615-0057, Expires 10/31/08

Department of Homeland Security
U.S. Citizenship and Immigration Services

N-600, Application for Certificate of Citizenship

Print clearly or type your answers, using CAPITAL letters in black ink. Failure to print clearly may delay processing of your application.

Part I. Information about you. *(Provide information about yourself, if you are a person applying for the Certificate of Citizenship. If you are a U.S. citizen parent applying for a Certificate of Citizenship for your minor child, provide information about your child).*

If your child has an "A" Number, write it here:

A

1. Current legal name
Family Name *(Last Name)*

Given Name *(First Name)*

Full Middle Name *(If applicable)*

2. Name exactly as it appears on your Permanent Resident Card *(If applicable).*
Family Name *(Last Name)*

Given Name *(First Name)*

Full Middle Name *(If applicable)*

3. Other names used since birth

Family Name *(Last Name)*	Given Name *(First Name)*	Middle Name *(If applicable)*

4. U.S. Social Security # *(If applicable)*

5. Date of Birth *(mm/dd/yyyy)*

6. Country of Birth

7. Country of Prior Nationality

8. Gender
☐ Male   ☐ Female

9. Height

For USCIS Use Only

Returned	Receipt
Date	
Date	
Resubmitted	
Date	
Date	
Reloc Sent	
Date	
Date	
Reloc Rec'd	
Date	
Date	

Remarks

Action Block

Part 2. Information about your eligibility. *(Check only one.)*

A. I am claiming U.S. citizenship through:

☐ A U.S. citizen father or a U.S. citizen mother.

☐ Both U.S. citizen parents.

☐ A U.S. citizen adoptive parent(s).

☐ An alien parent(s) who naturalized.

B. ☐ I am a U.S. citizen parent applying for a certificate of citizenship on behalf of my minor (under 18 years) **BIOLOGICAL** child.

C. ☐ I am a U.S. citizen parent applying for a certificate of citizenship on behalf of my minor (less than 18 years) **ADOPTED** child.

D. ☐ **Other** *(Please explain fully)*

To Be Completed by
☐ *Attorney or Representative,* if any.
Fill in box if G-28 is attached to represent the applicant.

ATTY State License #

Form N-600 (Rev. 10/15/07) Y

Part 3. Additional information about you. *(Provide additional information about **yourself**, if you are the person applying for the Certificate of Citizenship. If you are a U.S. citizen parent applying for a Certificate of Citizenship for your **minor child**, provide the additional information about your **minor child**).*

1. Home Address - Street Number and Name *(Do not write a P.O. Box in this space)*   Apartment Number

City	County	State/Province	Country	Zip/Postal Code

2. Mailing Address - Street Number and Name *(If different from home address)*   Apartment Number

City	County	State/Province	Country	Zip/Postal Code

3. Daytime Phone Number *(If any)*   Evening Phone Number *(If any)*   E-Mail Address *(If any)*

( )   ( )

4. Marital Status

☐ Single, Never Married   ☐ Married   ☐ Divorced   ☐ Widowed

☐ Marriage Annulled or Other *(Explain)*

5. Information about entry into the United States and current immigration status

   A. I arrived in the following manner:

   Port of Entry *(City/State)*   Date of Entry *(mm/dd/yyyy)*   Exact Name Used at Time of Entry:

   B. I used the following travel document to enter:

   ☐ Passport
   ☐ Passport Number   Country Issuing Passport   Date Passport Issued *(mm/dd/yyyy)*

   Other *(Please Specify Name of Document and Dates of Issuance)*

   C. I entered as:

   ☐ An immigrant (lawful permanent resident) using an immigrant visa
   ☐ A nonimmigrant
   ☐ A refugee
   ☐ Other *(Explain)*

   D. I obtained lawful permanent resident status through adjustment of status *(If applicable)*:

   Date you became a Permanent Resident *(mm/dd/yyyy)*   USCIS Office where granted adjustment of status

6. Have you previously applied for a certificate of citizenship or U.S. passport?   ☐ No   ☐ Yes *(Attach explanation)*

Part 3. Additional information about you. *(Provide additional information about **yourself**, if you are the person applying for the Certificate of Citizenship. If you are a U.S. citizen parent applying for a Certificate of Citizenship for your **minor child**, provide the additional information about your **minor child**). **Continued.***

7. **Were you adopted?** ☐ No ☐ Yes *(Please complete the following information):*

Date of Adoption *(mm/dd/yyyy)* Place of Final Adoption *(City/State or Country)*

Date Legal Custody Began *(mm/dd/yyyy)* Date Physical Custody Began *(mm/dd/yyyy)*

8. **Did you have to be re-adopted in the United States?** ☐ No ☐ Yes *(Please complete the following information):*

Date of Final Adoption *(mm/dd/yyyy)* Place of Final Adoption *(City/State)*

Date Legal Custody Began *(mm/dd/yyyy)* Date Physical Custody Began *(mm/dd/yyyy)*

9. **Were your parents married to each other when you were born (or adopted)?** ☐ No ☐ Yes

10. **Have you been absent from the United States since you first arrived?** *(Only for persons born before October 10, 1952, who are claiming U.S. citizenship at time of birth; otherwise, do not complete this section.)* ☐ No ☐ Yes

If yes, complete the following information about all absences, beginning with your most recent trip. If you need more space, use a separate sheet of paper.

Date You Left the United States *(mm/dd/yyyy)*	Date You Returned to the United States *(mm/dd/yyyy)*	Place of Entry Upon Return to the United States

Part 4. Information about U.S. citizen father (or adoptive father). *(Complete this section if you are claiming citizenship through a U.S. citizen father. If you are a U.S. citizen father applying for a Certificate of Citizenship on behalf of your minor biological or adopted child, provide information about **yourself** below.)*

1. **Current legal name of U.S. citizen father.**

Family Name *(Last Name)* Given Name *(First Name)* Full Middle Name *(If applicable)*

2. **Date of Birth** *(mm/dd/yyyy)* 3. **Country of Birth** 4. **Country of Nationality**

5. **Home Address** - Street Number and Name *(If deceased, so state and enter date of death.)* Apartment Number

City County State/Province Country Zip/Postal Code

Part 4. Information about U.S. citizen father (or adoptive father). *(Complete this section if you are claiming citizenship through a U.S. citizen father. If you are a U.S. citizen father applying for a Certificate of Citizenship on behalf of your minor biological or adopted child, provide information about **yourself** below.)* ***Continued.***

6. **U.S. citizen by:**

   ☐ Birth in the United States

   ☐ Birth abroad to U.S. citizen parent(s)

   ☐ Acquisition after birth through naturalization of alien parent(s)

   ☐ Naturalization

Date of Naturalization *(mm/dd/yyyy)*	Place of Naturalization *(Name of Court and City/State or USCIS or Former INS Office Location)*

Certificate of Naturalization Number	Former "A" Number *(If known)*

7. **Has your father ever lost U.S. citizenship or taken any action that would cause loss of U.S. citizenship?**

   ☐ No   ☐ Yes *(Provide full explanation on a separate sheet(s) of paper.)*

8. **Dates of Residence and/or Physical Presence in the United States** *(Complete this only if you are an applicant claiming U.S. citizenship at time of birth abroad)*

   Provide the dates your U.S. citizen father resided in or was physically present in the United States. If you need more space, use a separate sheet(s) of paper.

From *(mm/dd/yyyy)*	To *(mm/dd/yyyy)*

9. **Marital History**

   A. How many times has your U.S. citizen father been married (including annulled marriages)? [_____]

   B. Information about U.S. citizen father's **current spouse:**

Family Name *(Last Name)*	Given Name *(First Name)*	Full Middle Name *(If applicable)*

Date of Birth *(mm/dd/yyyy)*	Country of Birth	Country of Nationality

Home Address - Street Number and Name	Apartment Number

City	County	State or Province	Country	Zip/Postal Code

Date of Marriage *(mm/dd/yyyy)*	Place of Marriage *(City/State or Country)*

   Spouse's Immigration Status:

   ☐ U.S. Citizen   ☐ Lawful Permanent Resident   ☐ Other *(Explain)* [_____]

   C. Is your U.S. citizen father's current spouse also your mother?   ☐ No   ☐ Yes

Part 5. Information about your U.S. citizen mother (or adoptive mother). *(Complete this section if you are claiming citizenship through a U.S. citizen mother (or adoptive mother). If you are a U.S. citizen mother applying for a Certificate of Citizenship on behalf of your minor biological or adopted child, provide information about **yourself** below).*

1. **Current legal name of U.S. citizen mother.**

   Family Name *(Last Name)*   Given Name *(First Name)*   Full Middle Name *(If applicable)*

2. **Date of Birth** *(mm/dd/yyyy)*   3. **Country of Birth**   4. **Country of Nationality**

5. **Home Address** - Street Number and Name *(If deceased, so state and enter date of death)*   Apartment Number

   City   County   State/Province   Country   Zip/Postal Code

6. **U.S. citizen by:**

   ☐ Birth in the United States

   ☐ Birth abroad to U.S. citizen parent(s)

   ☐ Acquisition after birth through naturalization of alien parent(s)

   ☐ Naturalization

   Date of Naturalization *(mm/dd/yyyy)*   Place of Naturalization *(Name of Court and City/State or USCIS)*

   Certificate of Naturalization Number   Former "A" Number *(If known)*

7. **Has your mother ever lost U.S. citizenship or taken any action that would cause loss of U.S. citizenship?**

   ☐ No   ☐ Yes *(Provide full explanation on a separate sheet(s) of paper.)*

8. **Dates of Residence and/or Physical Presence in the United States** *(Complete this only if you are an applicant claiming U.S. citizenship at time of birth abroad)*

   Provide the dates your U.S. citizen father resided in or was physically present in the United States. If you need more space, use a separate sheet(s) of paper.

From *(mm/dd/yyyy)*	To *(mm/dd/yyyy)*

9. **Marital History**

   A. How many times has your U.S. citizen mother been married (including annulled marriages)?

   B. Information about U.S. citizen mother's **current spouse:**

   Family Name *(Last Name)*   Given Name *(First Name)*   Full Middle Name *(If applicable)*

   Date of Birth *(mm/dd/yyyy)*   Country of Birth   Country of Nationality

Part 5. Information about your U.S. citizen mother (or adoptive mother). *(Complete this section if you are claiming citizenship through a U.S. citizen mother (or adoptive mother). If you are a U.S. citizen mother applying for a Certificate of Citizenship on behalf of your minor biological or adopted child, provide information about **yourself** below). **Continued.***

C. Information about U.S. citizen mother's **current spouse**: *(Continued.)*

Home Address - Street Number and Name

Apartment Number

City	County	State or Province	Country	Zip/Postal Code

Date of Marriage *(mm/dd/yyyy)*   Place of Marriage *(City/State or Country)*

Spouse's Immigration Status:

☐ U.S. Citizen   ☐ Lawful Permanent Resident   ☐ Other *(Explain)*

D. Is your U.S. citizen mother's current spouse also your father?   ☐ No   ☐ Yes

Part 6. Information about military service of U. S. citizen parent(s). *(Complete this only if you are an applicant claiming U.S. citizenship at time of birth abroad.)*

1. Has your U. S. citizen parent(s) served in the armed forces?   ☐ No   ☐ Yes

2. If "Yes," which parent?   ☐ U.S. Citizen Father   ☐ U.S. Citizen Mother

3. Dates of Service. *(If time of service fulfills any of required physical presence, submit evidence of service.)*

From *(mm/dd/yyyy)*   To *(mm/dd/yyyy)*   From *(mm/dd/yyyy)*   To *(mm/dd/yyyy)*

4. Type of discharge.   ☐ Honorable   ☐ Other than Honorable   ☐ Dishonorable

Part 7. Signature.

I certify, under penalty of perjury under the laws of the United States, that this application and the evidence submitted with it is all true and correct. I authorize the release of any information from my records, or my minor child's records, that U.S. Citizenship and Immigration Services needs to determine eligibility for the benefit I am seeking.

Applicant's Signature   Printed Name   Date *(mm/dd/yyyy)*

Part 8. Signature of person preparing this form, if other than applicant.

I declare that I prepared this application at the request of the above person. The answers provided are based on information of which I have personal knowledge and/or were provided to me by the above-named person in response to the questions contained on this form.

Preparer's Signature   Preparer's Printed Name   Date *(mm/dd/yyyy)*

Name of Business/Organization *(If applicable)*   Preparer's Daytime Phone Number

( )

Preparer's Address - Street Number and Name

City	County	State	Zip Code

NOTE: Do not complete the following parts unless a USCIS officer instructs you to do so at the interview.

Part 9. Affidavit.

I, the (applicant, parent or legal guardian) _____ do swear or affirm, under penalty of perjury laws of the United States, that I know and understand the contents of this application signed by me, and the attached supplementary pages number (___) to (___) inclusive, that the same are true and correct to the best of my knowledge, and that corrections number (___) to (___) were made by me or at my request.

Signature of parent, guardian or applicant

Date *(mm/dd/yyyy)*

Subscribed and sworn or affirmed before me upon examination of the applicant (parent, guardian) on _____ at

Signature of Interviewing Officer

Title

Part 10. Officer Report and Recommendation on Application for Certificate of Citizenship.

On the basis of the documents, records and the testimony of persons examined, and the identification upon personal appearance of the underage beneficiary, I find that all the facts and conclusions set forth under oath in this application are ☐ true and correct; that the applicant did ☐ derive or acquire U.S. citizenship on _____ *(mm/dd/yyyy)*, through *(mark "X" in appropriate section of law or, if section of law not reflected, insert applicable section of law in "Other" block):* ☐ **section 301 of the INA**   ☐ **section 309 of the INA** ☐ **section 320 of the INA**   ☐ **section 321 of the INA**   ☐ **Other** _____

and that (s)he ☐ *has* ☐ *has not* been expatriated since that time. I recommend that this application be ☐ *granted* ☐ *denied* and that ☐ *A or* ☐ *AA* Certificate of Citizenship be issued in the name of _____ .

District Adjudication Officer's Name and Title

District Adjudication Officer's Signature

I do ☐ do not ☐ concur in recommendation of the application.

District Director or Officer-in-Charge Signature

Date *(mm/dd/yyyy)*

Department of Homeland Security
U.S. Citizenship and Immigration Services

OMB #1615-0012; Expires 11/30/07

I-130, Petition for Alien Relative

DO NOT WRITE IN THIS BLOCK - FOR USCIS OFFICE ONLY		
A#	Action Stamp	Fee Stamp

Section of Law/Visa Category
- [ ] 201(b) Spouse - IR-1/CR-1
- [ ] 201(b) Child - IR-2/CR-2
- [ ] 201(b) Parent - IR-5
- [ ] 203(a)(1) Unm. S or D - F1-1
- [ ] 203(a)(2)(A)Spouse - F2-1
- [ ] 203(a)(2)(A) Child - F2-2
- [ ] 203(a)(2)(B) Unm. S or D - F2-4
- [ ] 203(a)(3) Married S or D - F3-1
- [ ] 203(a)(4) Brother/Sister - F4-1

Petition was filed on: _____ (priority date)
- [ ] Personal Interview
- [ ] Pet. [ ] Ben. " A" File Reviewed
- [ ] Field Investigation
- [ ] 203(a)(2)(A) Resolved
- [ ] Previously Forwarded
- [ ] I-485 Filed Simultaneously
- [ ] 204(g) Resolved
- [ ] 203(g) Resolved

Remarks:

A. Relationship   You are the petitioner. Your relative is the beneficiary.

1. I am filing this petition for my:
- [ ] Husband/Wife [ ] Parent [ ] Brother/Sister [ ] Child

2. Are you related by adoption?
- [ ] Yes [ ] No

3. Did you gain permanent residence through adoption?
- [ ] Yes [ ] No

B. Information about you

1. Name (Family name in CAPS) (First) (Middle)

2. Address (Number and Street) (Apt. No.)

(Town or City) (State/Country) (Zip/Postal Code)

3. Place of Birth (Town or City) (State/Country)

4. Date of Birth **5. Gender** [ ] Male [ ] Female **6. Marital Status** [ ] Married [ ] Single [ ] Widowed [ ] Divorced

7. Other Names Used (including maiden name)

8. Date and Place of Present Marriage (if married)

9. U.S. Social Security (if any) **10. Alien Registration Number**

11. Name(s) of Prior Husband(s)/Wive(s) **12. Date(s) Marriage(s) Ended**

13. If you are a U.S. citizen, complete the following:
My citizenship was acquired through (check one):
- [ ] Birth in the U.S.
- [ ] Naturalization. Give certificate number and date and place of issuance.
- [ ] Parents. Have you obtained a certificate of citizenship in your own name?
  - [ ] Yes. Give certificate number, date and place of issuance. [ ] No

14. If you are a lawful permanent resident alien, complete the following:
Date and place of admission for or adjustment to lawful permanent residence and class of admission.

14b. Did you gain permanent resident status through marriage to a U.S. citizen or lawful permanent resident?
- [ ] Yes [ ] No

C. Information about your relative

1. Name (Family name in CAPS) (First) (Middle)

2. Address (Number and Street) (Apt. No.)

(Town or City) (State/Country) (Zip/Postal Code)

3. Place of Birth (Town or City) (State/Country)

4. Date of Birth **5. Gender** [ ] Male [ ] Female **6. Marital Status** [ ] Married [ ] Single [ ] Widowed [ ] Divorced

7. Other Names Used (including maiden name)

8. Date and Place of Present Marriage (if married)

9. U.S. Social Security (if any) **10. Alien Registration Number**

11. Name(s) of Prior Husband(s)/Wive(s) **12. Date(s) Marriage(s) Ended**

13. Has your relative ever been in the U.S.? [ ] Yes [ ] No

14. If your relative is currently in the U.S., complete the following:
He or she arrived as a:
(visitor, student, stowaway, without inspection, etc.)

Arrival/Departure Record (I-94) **Date arrived**

Date authorized stay expired, or will expire, as shown on Form I-94 or I-95

15. Name and address of present employer (if any)

Date this employment began

16. Has your relative ever been under immigration proceedings?
- [ ] No [ ] Yes Where _____ When _____
- [ ] Removal [ ] Exclusion/Deportation [ ] Rescission [ ] Judicial Proceedings

INITIAL RECEIPT	RESUBMITTED	RELOCATED: Rec'd	Sent	COMPLETED: Appv'd	Denied	Ret'd

Form I-130 (Rev. 07/30/07)Y

C. Information about your alien relative (continued)

17. List husband/wife and all children of your relative.

(Name)	(Relationship)	(Date of Birth)	(Country of Birth)

18. Address in the United States where your relative intends to live.

(Street Address)	(Town or City)	(State)

19. Your relative's address abroad. (Include street, city, province and country)   Phone Number (if any)

20. If your relative's native alphabet is other than Roman letters, write his or her name and foreign address in the native alphabet.

(Name)   Address (Include street, city, province and country):

21. If filing for your husband/wife, give last address at which you lived together. (Include street, city, province, if any, and country):

From: To:

22. Complete the information below if your relative is in the United States and will apply for adjustment of status.

Your relative is in the United States and will apply for adjustment of status to that of a lawful permanent resident at the USCIS office in:

If your relative is not eligible for adjustment of status, he or she will apply for a visa abroad at the American consular post in:

(City)	(State)	(City)	(Country

NOTE: Designation of an American embassy or consulate outside the country of your relative's last residence does not guarantee acceptance for processing by that post. Acceptance is at the discretion of the designated embassy or consulate.

D. Other information

1. If separate petitions are also being submitted for other relatives, give names of each and relationship.

2. Have you ever before filed a petition for this or any other alien?   ☐ Yes ☐ No

If "Yes," give name, place and date of filing and result.

WARNING: USCIS investigates claimed relationships and verifies the validity of documents. USCIS seeks criminal prosecutions when family relationships are falsified to obtain visas.

PENALTIES: By law, you may be imprisoned for not more than five years or fined $250,000, or both, for entering into a marriage contract for the purpose of evading any provision of the immigration laws. In addition, you may be fined up to $10,000 and imprisoned for up to five years, or both, for knowlingly and willfully falsifying or concealing a material fact or using any false document in submitting this petition.

YOUR CERTIFICATION: I certify, under penalty of perjury under the laws of the United States of America, that the foregoing is true and correct. Furthermore, I authorize the release of any information from my records that the U.S. Citizenship and Immigration Services needs to determine eligiblity for the benefit that I am seeking.

E. Signature of petitioner.

Date   Phone Number (   )

F. Signature of person preparing this form, if other than the petitioner.

I declare that I prepared this document at the request of the person above and that it is based on all information of which I have any knowledge.

Print Name _____   Signature _____   Date _____

Address _____   G-28 ID or VOLAG Number, if any.

Department of Homeland Security
U. S. Citizenship and Immigration Services

OMB No. 1615-0013; Expires 11/30/07

I-131, Application for Travel Document

DO NOT WRITE IN THIS BLOCK	FOR USCIS USE ONLY (except G-28 block below)	

Document Issued
- ☐ Reentry Permit
- ☐ Refugee Travel Document
- ☐ Single Advance Parole
- ☐ Multiple Advance Parole
- Valid to: _____

Action Block

Receipt

If Reentry Permit or Refugee Travel Document, mail to:
- ☐ Address in Part 1
- ☐ American embassy/consulate
  at: _____
- ☐ Overseas DHS office
  at: _____

☐ Document Hand Delivered

On _____ By _____

To be completed by Attorney/Representative, if any.
Attorney State License # _____

☐ Check box if G-28 is attached.

Part 1.   Information about you. *(Please type or print in black ink.)*

1. A # _____

2. Date of Birth *(mm/dd/yyyy)* _____

3. Class of Admission _____

4. Gender   Male ☐   Female ☐

5. Name *(Family name in capital letters)*   *(First)*   *(Middle)*

6. Address *(Number and Street)*   Apt. # _____

City   State or Province   Zip/Postal Code   Country

7. Country of Birth

8. Country of Citizenship

9. Social Security # *(if any.)*

Part 2.   Application type *(check one).*

a. ☐ I am a permanent resident or conditional resident of the United States and I am applying for a reentry permit.

b. ☐ I now hold U.S. refugee or asylee status and I am applying for a refugee travel document.

c. ☐ I am a permanent resident as a direct result of refugee or asylee status and I am applying for a refugee travel document.

d. ☐ I am applying for an advance parole document to allow me to return to the United States after temporary foreign travel.

e. ☐ I am outside the United States and I am applying for an advance parole document.

f. ☐ I am applying for an advance parole document for a person who is outside the United States. *If you checked box "f", provide the following information about that person:*

1. Name (Family name in capital letters)   *(First)*   *(Middle)*

2. Date of Birth *(mm/dd/yyyy)*

3. Country of Birth

4. Country of Citizenship

5. Address *(Number and Street)*   Apt. #   Daytime Telephone # *(area/country code)*

City   State or Province   Zip/Postal Code   Country

Part 3. Processing information.

1. Date of Intended Departure *(mm/dd/yyyy)*	2. Expected Length of Trip

3. Are you, or any person included in this application, now in exclusion, deportation, removal or recission proceedings? ☐ No ☐ Yes *(Name of DHS office):* [____]

If you are applying for an Advance Parole Document, skip to Part 7.

4. Have you ever before been issued a reentry permit or refugee travel? ☐ No ☐ Yes *(Give the following information*
 for the last document issued to you):

Date Issued *(mm/dd/yyyy):* [____]   Disposition *(attached, lost, etc.):* [____]

5. Where do you want this travel document sent? *(Check one)*

a. ☐ To the U.S. address shown in **Part 1** on the first page of this form.

b. ☐ To an American embassy or consulate at: City: [____] Country: [____]

c. ☐ To a DHS office overseas at: City: [____] Country: [____]

d. If you checked "b" or "c", where should the notice to pick up the travel document be sent?

   ☐ To the address shown in **Part 2** on the first page of this form.

   ☐ To the address shown below:

Address *(Number and Street)*		Apt. #	Daytime Telephone # *(area/country code)*

City	State or Province	Zip/Postal Code	Country

Part 4. Information about your proposed travel.

Purpose of trip. *If you need more room, continue on a seperate sheet(s) of paper.*	List the countries you intend to visit.

Part 5. Complete only if applying for a reentry permit.

Since becoming a permanent resident of the United States (or during the past five years, whichever is less) how much total time have you spent outside the United States?

☐ less than six months ☐ two to three years
☐ six months to one year ☐ three to four years
☐ one to two years ☐ more than four years

Since you became a permanent resident of the United States, have you ever filed a federal income tax return as a nonresident, or failed to file a federal income tax return because you considered yourself to be a nonresident? *(If "Yes," give details on a separate sheet(s) of paper.)* ☐ Yes ☐ No

Part 6. Complete only if applying for a refugee travel document.

1. Country from which you are a refugee or asylee: [____]

If you answer "Yes" to any of the following questions, you must explain on a separate sheet(s) of paper.

2. Do you plan to travel to the above named country?	☐ Yes ☐ No

3. Since you were accorded refugee/asylee status, have you ever:
  a. returned to the above named country?   ☐ Yes ☐ No
  b. applied for and/or obtained a national passport, passport renewal or entry permit of that country?   ☐ Yes ☐ No
  c. applied for and/or received any benefit from such country (for example, health insurance benefits).   ☐ Yes ☐ No

4. Since you were accorded refugee/asylee status, have you, by any legal procedure or voluntary act:
  a. reacquired the nationality of the above named country?   ☐ Yes ☐ No
  b. acquired a new nationality?   ☐ Yes ☐ No
  c. been granted refugee or asylee status in any other country?   ☐ Yes ☐ No

Part 7. Complete only if applying for advance parole.

On a separate sheet(s) of paper, please explain how you qualify for an advance parole document and what circumstances warrant issuance of advance parole. Include copies of any documents you wish considered. *(See instructions.)*

1. For how many trips do you intend to use this document? ☐ One trip ☐ More than one trip

2. If the person intended to receive an advance parole document is outside the United States, provide the location (city and country) of the American embassy or consulate or the DHS overseas office that you want us to notify.

City

Country

3. If the travel document will be delivered to an overseas office, where should the notice to pick up the document be sent:

☐ To the address shown in **Part 2** on the first page of this form.

☐ To the address shown below:

Address *(Number and Street)*   Apt. #   Daytime Telephone # *(area/country code)*

City   State or Province   Zip/Postal Code   Country

Part 8. Signature. *Read the information on penalties in the instructions before completing this section. If you are filing for a reentry permit or refugee travel document, you must be in the United States to file this application.*

I certify, under penalty of perjury under the laws of the United States of America, that this application and the evidence submitted with it are all true and correct. I authorize the release of any information from my records that the U.S. Citizenship and Immigration Services needs to determine eligibility for the benefit I am seeking.

Signature   **Date** *(mm/dd/yyyy)*   **Daytime Telephone Number** *(with area code)*

Please Note: If you do not completely fill out this form or fail to submit required documents listed in the instructions, you may not be found eligible for the requested document and this application may be denied.

Part 9. Signature of person preparing form, if other than the applicant. *(Sign below.)*

I declare that I prepared this application at the request of the applicant and it is based on all information of which I have knowledge.

Signature   Print or Type Your Name

Firm Name and Address   Daytime Telephone Number *(with area code)*

Fax Number *(if any.)*   Date *(mm/dd/yyyy)*

Department of Homeland Security
U.S. Citizenship and Immigration Services

Form I-140, Immigrant Petition for Alien Worker

START HERE - Please type or print in black ink.

For USCIS Use Only

Part 1. Information about the person or organization filing this petition. If an individual is filing, use the top name line. Organizations should use the second line.

Family Name (Last Name)　　Given Name (First Name)　　Full Middle Name

Company or Organization Name

Address: (Street Number and Name)　　Suite #

Attn:

City　　State/Province

Country　　Zip/Postal Code

IRS Tax #　　U.S. Social Security # *(if any)*　　E-Mail Address *(if any)*

Part 2. Petition type.

This petition is being filed for: *(Check one.)*

a. ☐ An alien of extraordinary ability.

b. ☐ An outstanding professor or researcher.

c. ☐ A multinational executive or manager.

d. ☐ A member of the professions holding an advanced degree or an alien of exceptional ability (who is NOT seeking a National Interest Waiver).

e. ☐ A professional (at a minimum, possessing a bachelor's degree or a foreign degree equivalent to a U.S. bachelor's degree) or a skilled worker (requiring at least two years of specialized training or experience).

f. ☐ (Reserved.)

g. ☐ Any other worker (requiring less than two years of training or experience).

h. ☐ Soviet Scientist.

i. ☐ An alien applying for a National Interest Waiver (who **IS** a member of the professions holding an advanced degree or an alien of exceptional ability).

Part 3. Information about the person you are filing for.

Family Name (Last Name)　　Given Name (First Name)　　Full Middle Name

Address: (Street Number and Name)　　Apt. #

C/O: (In Care Of)

City　　State/Province

Country　　Zip/Postal Code　　E-Mail Address *(if any)*

Daytime Phone # *(with area/country codes)*　　Date of Birth *(mm/dd/yyyy)*

City/Town/Village of Birth　　State/Province of Birth　　Country of Birth

Country of Nationality/Citizenship　　A # *(if any)*　　U.S. Social Security # *(if any)*

If in the U.S.

Date of Arrival *(mm/dd/yyyy)*　　I-94 # *(Arrival/Departure Document)*

Current Nonimmigrant Status　　Date Status Expires *(mm/dd/yyyy)*

For USCIS Use Only

Returned　　Receipt

Date

Date

Resubmitted

Date

Date

Reloc Sent

Date

Date

Reloc Rec'd

Date

Date

Classification:
☐ 203(b)(1)(A) Alien of Extraordinary Ability
☐ 203(b)(1)(B) Outstanding Professor or Researcher
☐ 203(b)(1)(C) Multi-National Executive or Manager
☐ 203(b)(2) Member of Professions w/Adv. Degree or Exceptional Ability
☐ 203(b)(3)(A)(i) Skilled Worker
☐ 203(b)(3)(A)(ii) Professional
☐ 203(b)(3)(A)(iii) Other Worker

Certification:
☐ National Interest Waiver (NIW)
☐ Schedule A, Group I
☐ Schedule A, Group II

Priority Date　　**Consulate**

Concurrent Filing:

☐ **I-485 filed concurrently.**

Remarks

Action Block

To Be Completed by
Attorney or Representative, if any.
☐ Fill in box if G-28 is attached to represent the applicant.

ATTY State License #

Part 4. Processing Information.

1. Please complete the following for the person named in **Part 3**: *(Check one)*

☐ Alien will apply for a visa abroad at the American Embassy or Consulate at:

City

Foreign Country

☐ Alien is in the United States and will apply for adjustment of status to that of lawful permanent resident.

Alien's country of current residence or, if now in the U.S., last permanent residence abroad.

2. If you provided a U.S. address in **Part 3**, print the person's foreign address:

3. If the person's native alphabet is other than Roman letters, write the person's foreign name and address in the native alphabet:

4. Are any other petition(s) or application(s) being filed with this Form I-140?   ☐ Form I-485   ☐ Form I-765

☐ No   ☐ Yes-(check all that apply)   ☐ Form I-131   ☐ Other - Attach an explanation.

5. Is the person you are filing for in removal proceedings?   ☐ No   ☐ Yes-Attach an explanation.

6. Has any immigrant visa petition ever been filed by or on behalf of this person?   ☐ No   ☐ Yes-Attach an explanation.

If you answered yes to any of these questions, please provide the case number, office location, date of decision and disposition of the decision on a separate sheet(s) of paper.

Part 5. Additional information about the petitioner.

1. Type of petitioner *(Check one.)*

☐ Employer   ☐ Self   ☐ Other (Explain, e.g., Permanent Resident, U.S. citizen or any other person filing on behalf of the alien.)

2. If a company, give the following:

Type of Business

Date Established *(mm/dd/yyyy)*

Current Number of Employees

Gross Annual Income

Net Annual Income

NAICS Code

DOL/ETA Case Number

3. If an individual, give the following:

Occupation

Annual Income

Part 6. Basic information about the proposed employment.

1. Job Title

2. SOC Code

3. Nontechnical Description of Job

4. Address where the person will work if different from address in **Part 1**.

5. Is this a full-time position?

☐ Yes   ☐ No

6. If the answer to **Number 5** is "No," how many hours per week for the position?

7. Is this a permanent position?

☐ Yes   ☐ No

8. Is this a new position?

☐ Yes   ☐ No

9. Wages per week

$

Part 7. Information on spouse and all children of the person for whom you are filing.

List husband/wife and all children related to the individual for whom the petition is being filed. Provide an attachment of additional family members, if needed.

Name (First/Middle/Last)	Relationship	Date of Birth (mm/dd/yyyy)	Country of Birth

Part 8. Signature. *Read the information on penalties in the instructions before completing this section. If someone helped you prepare this petition, he or she must complete Part 9.*

I certify, under penalty of perjury under the laws of the United States of America, that this petition and the evidence submitted with it are all true and correct. I authorize U.S. Citizenship and Immigration Services to release to other government agencies any information from my USCIS (or former INS) records, if USCIS determines that such action is necessary to determine eligibility for the benefit sought.

Petitioner's Signature   **Daytime Phone Number** (Area/Country Codes)   **E-Mail Address**

Print Name   **Date** (mm/dd/yyyy)

NOTE: *If you do not fully complete this form or fail to submit the required documents listed in the instructions, a final decision on your petition may be delayed or the petition may be denied.*

Part 9. Signature of person preparing form, if other than above. *(Sign below.)*

I declare that I prepared this petition at the request of the above person and it is based on all information of which I have knowledge.

Attorney or Representative: In the event of a Request for Evidence (RFE), may the USCIS contact you by Fax or E-mail? ☐ Yes ☐ No

Signature   **Print Name**   **Date** (mm/dd/yyyy)

Firm Name and Address

Daytime Phone Number (Area/Country Codes)   **Fax Number** (Area/Country Codes)   **E-Mail Address**

Department of Homeland Security
U.S. Citizenship and Immigration Services

I-485, Application to Register
Permanent Residence or Adjust Status

START HERE - Please type or print in black ink.

Part 1. Information about you.

Family Name

Given Name

Middle Name

Address- C/O

Street Number and Name

Apt. #

City

State

Zip Code

Date of Birth *(mm/dd/yyyy)*

Country of Birth:

Country of Citizenship/Nationality:

U.S. Social Security #

A # *(if any)*

Date of Last Arrival *(mm/dd/yyyy)*

I-94 #

Current USCIS Status

Expires on *(mm/dd/yyyy)*

For USCIS Use Only

Returned	Receipt

Resubmitted	

Reloc Sent	

Reloc Rec'd	

Applicant Interviewed	

Part 2. Application type. *(Check one.)*

I am applying for an adjustment to permanent resident status because:

a. ☐ an immigrant petition giving me an immediately available immigrant visa number has been approved. (Attach a copy of the approval notice, or a relative, special immigrant juvenile or special immigrant military visa petition filed with this application that will give you an immediately available visa number, if approved.)

b. ☐ my spouse or parent applied for adjustment of status or was granted lawful permanent residence in an immigrant visa category that allows derivative status for spouses and children.

c. ☐ I entered as a K-1 fiancé(e) of a United States citizen whom I married within 90 days of entry, or I am the K-2 child of such a fiancé(e). (Attach a copy of the fiancé(e) petition approval notice and the marriage certificate).

d. ☐ I was granted asylum or derivative asylum status as the spouse or child of a person granted asylum and am eligible for adjustment.

e. ☐ I am a native or citizen of Cuba admitted or paroled into the United States after January 1, 1959, and thereafter have been physically present in the United States for at least one year.

f. ☐ I am the husband, wife or minor unmarried child of a Cuban described above in (e) and I am residing with that person, and was admitted or paroled into the United States after January 1, 1959, and thereafter have been physically present in the United States for at least one year.

g. ☐ I have continuously resided in the United States since before January 1, 1972.

h. ☐ Other basis of eligibility. Explain (for example, I was admitted as a refugee, my status has not been terminated, and I have been physically present in the U.S. for one year after admission). If additional space is needed, use a separate piece of paper.

I am already a permanent resident and am applying to have the date I was granted permanent residence adjusted to the date I originally arrived in the United States as a nonimmigrant or parolee, or as of May 2, 1964, whichever date is later, and: *(Check one.)*

i. ☐ I am a native or citizen of Cuba and meet the description in (e) above.

j. ☐ I am the husband, wife or minor unmarried child of a Cuban, and meet the description in (f) above.

Section of Law

☐ Sec. 209(b), INA
☐ Sec. 13, Act of 9/11/57
☐ Sec. 245, INA
☐ Sec. 249, INA
☐ Sec. 1 Act of 11/2/66
☐ Sec. 2 Act of 11/2/66
☐ Other

Country Chargeable

Eligibility Under Sec. 245

☐ Approved Visa Petition
☐ Dependent of Principal Alien
☐ Special Immigrant
☐ Other

Preference

Action Block

To be Completed by
Attorney or Representative, **if any**
☐ Fill in box if G-28 is attached to represent the applicant.

VOLAG #

ATTY State License #

Form I-485 (Rev. 07/30/07) Y

Part 3. Processing information.

A. City/Town/Village of Birth	Current Occupation
Your Mother's First Name	Your Father's First Name

Give your name exactly as it appears on your Arrival/Departure Record (Form I-94)

Place of Last Entry Into the United States *(City/State)*	In what status did you last enter? *(Visitor, student, exchange alien, crewman, temporary worker, without inspection, etc.)*
Were you inspected by a U.S. Immigration Officer? ☐ Yes ☐ No	
Nonimmigrant Visa Number	Consulate Where Visa Was Issued

Date Visa Was Issued (mm/dd/yyyy)	Gender: ☐ Male ☐ Female	Marital Status: ☐ Married ☐ Single ☐ Divorced ☐ Widowed

Have you ever before applied for permanent resident status in the U.S.?   ☐ No   ☐ Yes. If you checked "Yes," give date and place of filing and final disposition.

B. List your present husband/wife, all of your sons and daughters (If you have none, write "none." If additional space is needed, use separate paper.)

Family Name	Given Name	Middle Initial	Date of Birth *(mm/dd/yyyy)*
Country of Birth	Relationship	A #	Applying with you? ☐ Yes ☐ No
Family Name	Given Name	Middle Initial	Date of Birth *(mm/dd/yyyy)*
Country of Birth	Relationship	A #	Applying with you? ☐ Yes ☐ No
Family Name	Given Name	Middle Initial	Date of Birth *(mm/dd/yyyy)*
Country of Birth	Relationship	A #	Applying with you? ☐ Yes ☐ No
Family Name	Given Name	Middle Initial	Date of Birth *(mm/dd/yyyy)*
Country of Birth	Relationship	A #	Applying with you? ☐ Yes ☐ No
Family Name	Given Name	Middle Initial	Date of Birth *(mm/dd/yyyy)*
Country of Birth	Relationship	A #	Applying with you? ☐ Yes ☐ No

C. List your present and past membership in or affiliation with every organization, association, fund, foundation, party, club, society or similar group in the United States or in other places since your 16th birthday. Include any foreign military service in this part. If none, write "none." Include the name(s) of organization(s), location(s), dates of membership, from and to, and the nature of the organization(s). If additional space is needed, use a separate piece of paper.

Part 3. Processing information. *(Continued)*

Please answer the following questions. (If your answer is **"Yes"** on any one of these questions, explain on a separate piece of paper and refer to "What Are the General Filing Instructions? Initial Evidence" to determine what documentation to include with your application. Answering **"Yes"** does not necessarily mean that you are not entitled to adjust status or register for permanent residence.)

1. Have you ever, in or outside the United States:

   a. knowingly committed any crime of moral turpitude or a drug-related offense for which you have not been arrested? ☐ Yes ☐ No

   b. been arrested, cited, charged, indicted, fined or imprisoned for breaking or violating any law or ordinance, excluding traffic violations? ☐ Yes ☐ No

   c. been the beneficiary of a pardon, amnesty, rehabilitation decree, other act of clemency or similar action? ☐ Yes ☐ No

   d. exercised diplomatic immunity to avoid prosecution for a criminal offense in the United States? ☐ Yes ☐ No

2. Have you received public assistance in the United States from any source, including the United States government or any state, county, city or municipality (other than emergency medical treatment), or are you likely to receive public assistance in the future? ☐ Yes ☐ No

3. Have you ever:

   a. within the past ten years been a prostitute or procured anyone for prostitution, or intend to engage in such activities in the future? ☐ Yes ☐ No

   b. engaged in any unlawful commercialized vice, including, but not limited to, illegal gambling? ☐ Yes ☐ No

   c. knowingly encouraged, induced, assisted, abetted or aided any alien to try to enter the United States illegally? ☐ Yes ☐ No

   d. illicitly trafficked in any controlled substance, or knowingly assisted, abetted or colluded in the illicit trafficking of any controlled substance? ☐ Yes ☐ No

4. Have you ever engaged in, conspired to engage in, or do you intend to engage in, or have you ever solicited membership or funds for, or have you through any means ever assisted or provided any type of material support to any person or organization that has ever engaged or conspired to engage in sabotage, kidnapping, political assassination, hijacking or any other form of terrorist activity? ☐ Yes ☐ No

5. Do you intend to engage in the United States in:

   a. espionage? ☐ Yes ☐ No

   b. any activity a purpose of which is opposition to, or the control or overthrow of, the government of the United States, by force, violence or other unlawful means? ☐ Yes ☐ No

   c. any activity to violate or evade any law prohibiting the export from the United States of goods, technology or sensitive information? ☐ Yes ☐ No

6. Have you ever been a member of, or in any way affiliated with, the Communist Party or any other totalitarian party? ☐ Yes ☐ No

7. Did you, during the period from March 23, 1933 to May 8, 1945, in association with either the Nazi Government of Germany or any organization or government associated or allied with the Nazi Government of Germany, ever order, incite, assist or otherwise participate in the persecution of any person because of race, religion, national origin or political opinion? ☐ Yes ☐ No

8. Have you ever engaged in genocide, or otherwise ordered, incited, assisted or otherwise participated in the killing of any person because of race, religion, nationality, ethnic origin or political opinion? ☐ Yes ☐ No

9. Have you ever been deported from the United States, or removed from the United States at government expense, excluded within the past year, or are you now in exclusion, deportation, removal or recission proceedings? ☐ Yes ☐ No

10. Are you under a final order of civil penalty for violating section 274C of the Immigration and Nationality Act for use of fraudulent documents or have you, by fraud or willful misrepresentation of a material fact, ever sought to procure, or procured, a visa, other documentation, entry into the United States or any immigration benefit? ☐ Yes ☐ No

11. Have you ever left the United States to avoid being drafted into the U.S. Armed Forces? ☐ Yes ☐ No

12. Have you ever been a J nonimmigrant exchange visitor who was subject to the two-year foreign residence requirement and have not yet complied with that requirement or obtained a waiver? ☐ Yes ☐ No

13. Are you now withholding custody of a U.S. citizen child outside the United States from a person granted custody of the child? ☐ Yes ☐ No

14. Do you plan to practice polygamy in the United States? ☐ Yes ☐ No

Part 4. **Signature.** *(Read the information on penalties in the instructions before completing this section. You must file this application while in the United States.)*

Your registration with U.S. Citizenship and Immigration Services.

"I understand and acknowledge that, under section 262 of the Immigration and Nationality Act (Act), as an alien who has been or will be in the United States for more than 30 days, I am required to register with U.S. Citizenship and Immigration Services. I understand and acknowledge that, under section 265 of the Act, I am required to provide USCIS with my current address and written notice of any change of address within **ten** days of the change. I understand and acknowledge that USCIS will use the most recent address that I provide to USCIS, on any form containing these acknowledgements, for all purposes, including the service of a Notice to Appear should it be necessary for USCIS to initiate removal proceedings against me. I understand and acknowledge that if I change my address without providing written notice to USCIS, I will be held responsible for any communications sent to me at the most recent address that I provided to USCIS. I further understand and acknowledge that, if removal proceedings are initiated against me and I fail to attend any hearing, including an initial hearing based on service of the Notice to Appear at the most recent address that I provided to USCIS or as otherwise provided by law, I may be ordered removed in my absence, arrested and removed from the United States."

Selective Service Registration.

The following applies to you if you are a male at least 18 years old, but not yet 26 years old, who is required to register with the Selective Service System: "I understand that my filing this adjustment of status application with U.S. Citizenship and Immigration Services authorizes USCIS to provide certain registration information to the Selective Service System in accordance with the Military Selective Service Act. Upon USCIS acceptance of my application, I authorize USCIS to transmit to the Selective Service System my name, current address, Social Security Number, date of birth and the date I filed the application for the purpose of recording my Selective Service registration as of the filing date. If, however, USCIS does not accept my application, I further understand that, if so required, I am responsible for registering with the Selective Service by other means, provided I have not yet reached age 26."

Applicant's Certification

I certify, under penalty of perjury under the laws of the United States of America, that this application and the evidence submitted with it is all true and correct. I authorize the release of any information from my records that U.S. Citizenship and Immigration Services (USCIS) needs to determine eligibility for the benefit I am seeking.

Signature	Print Your Name	Date	Daytime Phone Number
			( )

NOTE: *If you do not completely fill out this form or fail to submit required documents listed in the instructions, you may not be found eligible for the requested document and this application may be denied.*

Part 5. Signature of person preparing form, if other than above. (sign below)

I declare that I prepared this application at the request of the above person and it is based on all information of which I have knowledge.

Signature	Print Your Full Name	Date	Phone Number (Include Area Code)
			( )

Firm Name and Address		E-Mail Address (if any)	

Department of Homeland Security
U.S. Citizenship and Immigration Services

I-539, Application to Extend/ Change Nonimmigrant Status

START HERE - Please type or print in black ink.

For USCIS Use Only

Part 1. Information about you

Family Name	Given Name	Middle Name

Address -
In care of -

Street Number and Name		Apt. #

City	State	Zip Code	Daytime Phone #

Country of Birth	Country of Citizenship

Date of Birth (mm/dd/yyyy)	U. S. Social Security # (if any)	A # (if any)

Date of Last Arrival Into the U.S.	I-94 #

Current Nonimmigrant Status	Expires on (mm/dd/yyyy)

For USCIS Use Only

Returned	Receipt
Date	
Resubmitted	
Date	
Reloc Sent	
Date	
Reloc Rec'd	
Date	

Part 2. Application type *(See instructions for fee.)*

1. I am applying for: *(Check one.)*

a. ☐ An extension of stay in my current status.
b. ☐ A change of status. The new status I am requesting is: _____
c. ☐ Reinstatement to student status

2. Number of people included in this application: *(Check one.)*

a. ☐ I am the only applicant.
b. ☐ Members of my family are filing this application with me.
The total number of people (including me) in the application is:
(Complete the supplement for each co-applicant.) _____

☐ Applicant Interviewed on

_____
Date

☐ *Extension Granted to (Date):*

_____

Change of Status/Extension Granted
New Class: From *(Date)*: _____
_____ To *(Date)*: _____

Part 3. Processing information

1. I/We request that my/our current or requested status be extended until (mm/dd/yyyy): _____

2. Is this application based on an extension or change of status already granted to your spouse, child, or parent?
☐ No ☐ Yes. USCIS Receipt # _____

3. Is this application based on a separate petition or application to give your spouse, child, or parent an extension or change of status? ☐ No ☐ Yes, filed with this I-539.

☐ Yes, filed previously and pending with USCIS. Receipt #: _____

4. If you answered "Yes" to Question 3, give the name of the petitioner or applicant:

If the petition or application is pending with USCIS, also give the following data:

Office filed at	Filed on (mm/dd/yyyy)

If Denied:
☐ Still within period of stay
☐ S/D to: _____
☐ Place under docket control

Remarks:

Action Block

Part 4. Additional information

1. For applicant #1, provide passport information: | Valid to: (mm/dd/yyyy)
Country of Issuance

2. Foreign Address: Street Number and Name	Apt. #

City or Town	State or Province

Country	Zip/Postal Code

To Be Completed by
Attorney or Representative, if any

☐ Fill in box if G-28 is attached to represent the applicant.

ATTY State License #

3. Answer the following questions. If you answer "Yes" to any question, please describe the circumstances in detail and explain on a separate sheet(s) of paper.

		Yes	No
a.	Are you, or any other person included on the application, an applicant for an immigrant visa?	☐	☐
b.	Has an immigrant petition ever been filed for you or for any other person included in this application?	☐	☐
c.	Has a Form I-485, Application to Register Permanent Residence or Adjust Status, ever been filed by you or by any other person included in this application?	☐	☐
d. 1.	Have you or any other person, included in this application, ever been arrested or convicted of any criminal offense since last entering the United States?	☐	☐

d. 2. Have you EVER ordered, incited, called for, commited, assisted, helped with, or otherwise participated in any of the following:

(a) Acts involving torture or genocide?

(b) Killing any person?

(c) Intentionally and severely injuring any person?

(d) Engaging in any kind of sexual contact or relations with any person who was being forced or threatened?

(e) Limiting or denying any person's ability to exercise religious beliefs?   ☐   ☐

d. 3. Have you EVER:

(a) Served in, been a member of, assisted in, or participated in any military unit, paramilitary unit, police unit, self-defense unit, vigilante unit, rebel group, guerrilla group, militia, or insurgent organization?

(b) Served in any prison, jail, prison camp, detention facility, labor camp, or any other situation that involved detaining persons?   ☐   ☐

d. 4. Have you EVER been a member of, assisted in, or participated in any group, unit, or organization of any kind in which you or other persons used any type of weapon against any person or threatened to do so?   ☐   ☐

d. 5. Have you EVER assisted or participated in selling or providing weapons to any person who to your knowledge used them against another person, or in transporting weapons to any person who to your knowledge used them against another person?   ☐   ☐

d. 6. Have you EVER received any type of military, paramilitary, or weapons training?   ☐   ☐

e.	Have you, or any other person included in this application, done anything that violated the terms of the nonimmigrant status you now hold?	☐	☐
f.	Are you, or any other person included in this application, now in removal proceedings?	☐	☐
g.	Have you, or any other person included in this application, been employed in the United States since last admitted or granted an extension or change of status?	☐	☐

1. If you answered "Yes" to Question 3f, give the following information concerning the removal proceedings on the attached page entitled "**Part 4. Additional information. Page for answers to 3f and 3g.**" Include the name of the person in removal proceedings and information on jurisdiction, date proceedings began, and status of proceedings.

2. If you answered "No" to Question 3g, fully describe how you are supporting yourself on the attached page entitled "**Part 4. Additional information. Page for answers to 3f and 3g.**" Include the source, amount, and basis for any income.

3. If you answered "Yes" to Question 3g, fully describe the employment on the attached page entitled "**Part 4. Additional information. Page for answers to 3f and 3g.**" Include the name of the person employed, name and address of the employer, weekly income, and whether the employment was specifically authorized by USCIS.

		Yes	No
h.	Are you currently or have you ever been a J-1 exchange visitor or a J-2 dependent of a J-1 exchange visitor?	☐	☐

If yes, you must provide the dates you maintained status as a J-1 exchange visitor or J-2 dependent. Willful failure to disclose this information (or other relevant information) can result in your application being denied. Also, please provide proof of your J-1 or J-2 status, such as a copy of Form DS-2019, Certificate of Eligibility for Exchange Visitor Status, or a copy of your passport that includes the J visa stamp.

Part 5. Applicant's Statement and Signature *(Read the information on penalties in the instructions before completing this section. You must file this application while in the United States).*

Applicant's Statement (Check One):

☐ I can read and understand English, and have read and understand each and every question and instruction on this form, as well as my answer to each question.

☐ Each and every question and instruction on this form, as well as my answer to each question, has been read to me by the person named below in _____, a language in which I am fluent. I understand each and every question and instruction on this form, as well as my answer to each question.

Applicant's Signature

I certify, under penalty of perjury under the laws of the United States of America, that this application and the evidence submitted with it is all true and correct. I authorize the release of any information from my records that U.S. Citizenship and Immigration Services needs to determine eligibility for the benefit I am seeking.

Signature	Print your Name	Date
Daytime Telephone Number	E-Mail Address	

NOTE: *If you do not completely fill out this form or fail to submit required documents listed in the instructions, you may not be found eligible for the requested benefit and this application may be denied.*

Part 6. Interpreter's Statement

Language used: _____

I certify that I am fluent in English and the above-mentioned language. I further certify that I have read each and every question and instruction on this form, as well as the answer to each question, to this applicant in the above-mentioned language, and the applicant has understood each and every instruction and question on the form, as well as the answer to each question.

Signature	Print Your Name	Date
Firm Name (If Applicable)	Daytime Telephone Number *(Area Code and Number)*	
Address	Fax Number *(Area Code and Number)*	E-Mail Address

Part 7. Signature of Person Preparing Form, if Other than Above *(Sign Below)*

Signature	Print Your Name	Date
Firm Name (If Applicable)	Daytime Telephone Number *(Area Code and Number)*	
Address	Fax Number *(Area Code and Number)*	E-Mail Address

I declare that I prepared this application at the request of the above person and it is based on all information of which I have knowledge.

Part 4. (Continued) Additional information. Page for answers to 3f and 3g.

If you answered "Yes" to Question 3f in Part 4 on Page 3 of this form, give the following information concerning the removal proceedings. Include the name of the person in removal proceedings and information on jurisdiction, date proceedings began, and status of proceedings.

If you answered "No" to Question 3g in Part 4 on Page 3 of this form, fully describe how you are supporting yourself. Include the source, amount and basis for any income.

If you answered "Yes" to Question 3g in Part 4 on Page 3 of this form, fully describe the employment. Include the name of the person employed, name and address of the employer, weekly income, and whether the employment was specifically authorized by USCIS.

Supplement -1
Attach to Form I-539 when more than one person is included in the petition or application.
(List each person separately. Do not include the person named in the Form I-539.)

Family Name	Given Name	Middle Name	Date of Birth (mm/dd/yyyy)
Country of Birth	Country of Citizenship	U.S. Social Security # (if any)	A # (if any)
Date of Arrival (mm/dd/yyyy)		I-94 #	
Current Nonimmigrant Status:		Expires on (mm/dd/yyyy)	
Country Where Passport Issued		Expiration Date (mm/dd/yyyy)	

Family Name	Given Name	Middle Name	Date of Birth (mm/dd/yyyy)
Country of Birth	Country of Citizenship	U.S. Social Security # (if any)	A # (if any)
Date of Arrival (mm/dd/yyyy)		I-94 #	
Current Nonimmigrant Status:		Expires on (mm/dd/yyyy)	
Country Where Passport Issued		Expiration Date (mm/dd/yyyy)	

Family Name	Given Name	Middle Name	Date of Birth (mm/dd/yyyy)
Country of Birth	Country of Citizenship	U.S. Social Security # (if any)	A # (if any)
Date of Arrival (mm/dd/yyyy)		I-94 #	
Current Nonimmigrant Status:		Expires on (mm/dd/yyyy)	
Country Where Passport Issued		Expiration Date (mm/dd/yyyy)	

Family Name	Given Name	Middle Name	Date of Birth (mm/dd/yyyy)
Country of Birth	Country of Citizenship	U.S. Social Security # (if any)	A # (if any)
Date of Arrival (mm/dd/yyyy)		I-94 #	
Current Nonimmigrant Status:		Expires on (mm/dd/yyyy)	
Country Where Passport Issued		Expiration Date (mm/dd/yyyy)	

Family Name	Given Name	Middle Name	Date of Birth (mm/dd/yyyy)
Country of Birth	Country of Citizenship	U.S. Social Security # (if any)	A # (if any)
Date of Arrival (mm/dd/yyyy)		I-94 #	
Current Nonimmigrant Status:		Expires on (mm/dd/yyyy)	
Country Where Passport Issued		Expiration Date (mm/dd/yyyy)	

If you need additional space, attach a separate sheet(s) of paper.
Place your name, A #, if any, date of birth, form number, and application date at the top of the sheet(s) of paper.

U.S. Citizenship
and Immigration
Services

USCIS Is Making Photos Simpler

Washington, DC — In accordance with language specified in the Border Security Act of 2003, U.S. Citizenship and Immigration Services (USCIS) announced a change in the photo requirements for all applicants from a three-quarter face position to a standard, full-frontal face position to take effect **August 2, 2004**.

USCIS will accept both three-quarter and full-frontal color photographs until **September 1, 2004,** after which only full-frontal color will be accepted.

The application process of customers who have already submitted materials that include color photos with the three-quarter standard **will not** be affected by this change.

All photos must be of just the person. Where more than one photo is required, all photos of the person must be identical. All photos must meet the specifications for full-frontal/passport photos.

For more information on photo standards, visit the Department of State website at http://www.travel.state.gov/passport/pptphotos/index.html, or contact the USCIS National Customer Service Center at 1 800 375 5283.

List of forms that require photos is on the back

Old Three-Quarter Style Photo

New Passport Style Photo

Photos Must Be in Color

M-603 (07/04)

2 photos are required for the following forms:

I-90 – Renew or replace your Permanent Resident Card (green card)

I-131 – Re-entry permit, refugee travel document, or advance parole

I-485 – Adjust status and become a permanent resident while in the U.S.

I-765 – Employment Authorization/Employment Authorization Document (EAD)

I-777 – Replace Northern Mariana Card

I-821 – Temporary Protected Status (TPS) Program

N-300 – Declaration of Intent (to apply for U.S. citizenship)

N-400 – Naturalization (to become a U.S. citizen)

N-565 – Replace Naturalization/Citizenship Certificate

3 photos are required for the following forms:

I-698 – Temporary Resident's application under the 1987 Legalization Program for permanent resident status — file 1 photo for your application, and bring the other 2 with you to your interview

N-600K – To apply for U.S. citizenship for foreign-born child residing abroad with U.S. citizen parent

4 photos are required for the following forms:

I-817 – To apply for Family Unity Benefits

I-881 – NACARA — suspension of deportation or special rule cancellation

File the following with your photos and of others as shown below:

I-129F – Fiancé(e) Petition — file with 1 photo of you + 1 photo of fiancé(e)

I-130 – Relative petition — if filing for your husband or wife, file with 1 photo of you + 1 photo of your husband or wife

I-589 – Asylum — file with 1 photo of you + 1 photo of each family member listed in Part A. II that you are including in your application

I-730 – Relative petition filed by a person granted Asylum or Refugee status — file with 1 photo of the family member for whom you are filing the I-730

I-914 – 'T' nonimmigrant status — file with 3 photos of you + 3 photos of each immediate family member for which you file an I-914A supplement

All photos must be of just the person. Where more than one photo is required, all photos of the person must be identical. All photos must meet the specifications for full-frontal/passport photos.

For more information, visit our website at www.uscis.gov, or call our customer service at 1 800 375 5283.

Siglas y abreviaciones

La lista siguiente contiene definiciones para muchas siglas y abreviaciones que se encuentran en el papeleo y los recursos que podrías utilizar a través del proceso. (Gracias a la página de Web de USCIS: www.uscis.gov.)

A

ACE	Accelerated Citizen Examination
ADIT	Alien Documentation, Identification and Telecommunication System
A File	Basic Alien File (contains Alien number)
AILA	American Immigration Lawyers Association
ARC	Alien Registration Card (Green Card)
ASC	Application Support Center (Naturalization)
ASVI	Alien Status Verification Index

B

BCC	Border Crossing Card (Mexico)
BCIC	Border Crossing Identification Card (I-586)
BHRHA	Bureau of Human Rights and Humanitarian Affairs

BIA   Board of Immigration Appeals
BP   Border Patrol
BSC   Baltimore Service Center

C
CAP   Citizens Advisory Panel
CAP   Cuban Adjustment Program
CBOs   Community-Based Organizations
CBIC   Canadian Border Intelligence Center
CFR   Code of Federal Regulations
CIJ   Chief Immigration Judge
CIMT   Crimes Involving Moral Turpitude
CIS   Central Index System
CPS   Current Population Survey (Census)
CUSA   Citizenship U.S.A.

D
DDP   Detention and Deportation Program
DED   Deferred Enforced Departure
DFS   Designated Fingerprint Service
DOE   Date of Entry
DOL   Department of Labor
DOS   Department of State

E
EAD   Employment Authorization Document
EFOIA   Electronic Freedom of Information Act Initiative
EOIR   Executive Office for Immigration Review

F
FCC   Fingerprint Clearance Coordination Center
FD-258   Fingerprint Card
FLSA   Fair Labor Standard Act
FOIA/PA   Freedom of Information Act/Privacy Act
FRC   Federal Records Centers

G
GREEN CARD   Alien Registration Receipt Card (Form I-151 or I-551)

H
HRO   Human Resource Office

I
IA   Immigration Agent
IAO   Office of International Affairs
ICF   Immigration Card Facility (Arlington, TX)

IDENT	Automated Fingerprint Identification System
IDP	In District Processing
IE	Immigration Examiner
II	Immigration Inspector
IIO	Immigration Information Officer
IIRIRA	Illegal Immigration Reform and Immigrant Responsibility Act
IJ	Immigration Judge
INA	Immigration and Nationality Act
IO	Immigration Officer
IRCA	Immigration Reform and Control Act of 1986

L

LAPR	Lawfully Admitted for Permanent Residence
LAW	Legally Authorized (or Admitted) Worker
LPR	Lawful Permanent Resident
LULAC	League of United Latin American Citizens

M

MIRP	Mexican Interior Repatriation Program

N

NACS	Naturalization Automated Casework System
NATZ	Naturalization
NGOs	Non-Governmental Organizations
NINSC	National INS Council
NIV	Non-Immigrant Visa
NRC	National Records Center
NSC	Nebraska Service Center (Lincoln)
NTA	Notice to Appear
NVC	National Visa Center (Department of State)

O

OIL	Office of Immigration Litigation
ONO	Office of Naturalization Operations

P

PHS	Public Health Services
POE	Port-of-Entry
PRC	Permanent Resident Card

R

RTD	Refugee Travel Document

S

SAW	Special Agricultural Workers
SIO	Special Inquiry Officer (Immigration Judge)

SPC	Service Processing Center
SW	Southwest

T

TAPS	Telephone Application Processing System
TSC	Texas Service Center (Irving)
TRWOV	Transit Without Visa

U

UNHCR	United Nations High Commissioner for Refugees
USC	U.S. Citizen
USCS	United States Customs Service

V

VD	Voluntary Departure
VR	Voluntary Return
VSC	Vermont Service Center (St. Albans)
VWPP	Visa Waiver Pilot Program

W

WRO	Western Region Office (Laguna Niguel, CA)